101
CHICKEN
RECIPES

A Collection of Your Favorites

PUBLICATIONS INTERNATIONAL, LTD.

Nutritional Analysis: The nutritional information that appears with each recipe was submitted in part by the participating companies and associations. Every effort has been made to check the accuracy of these numbers. However, because numerous variables account for a wide range of values for certain foods, nutritive analyses in this book should be considered approximate.

Microwave Cooking: Microwave ovens vary in wattage. Use the cooking times as guidelines and check for doneness before adding more time.

101 CHICKEN RECIPES

A Collection of Your Favorites

Basic
Chicken Facts • 4

Hearty
Soups, Salads & Sandwiches • 12

Sizzling
Stir-Fry Meals • 34

Homey
Casserole Favorites • 52

Terrific
One-Dish Meals • 74

Tasty
Roasting, Grilling & More • 100

Quick
Meals from 6 Ingredients • 136

Savory
Light Dinners • 162

Acknowledgments • 184

Index • 185

Basic

CHICKEN FACTS

Chicken is one of the most popular foods available in today's supermarkets. First, it is versatile. Chicken can be prepared using a variety of cooking methods, such as braising, broiling, frying, grilling, roasting and sautéing, and its mild taste combines well with a wide variety of flavors. However, what appeals to many cooks is the convenience of chicken, especially quick-to-fix boneless chicken breasts and easy-roasting whole chickens. In addition, whole and cut-up chickens, drumsticks and wings are inexpensive protein sources. For those people who are trying to reduce their fat consumption, skinless chicken breasts trimmed of fat are a perfect choice. With all of this going for it and a delicious flavor as well, it's no wonder that chicken is a mainstay in every American kitchen.

Types and Cuts

Chickens are classified by age. Young chickens are tender and cook quickly; older chickens need slow, moist cooking to make them tender. For best results, it is important to know which type of chicken to buy.

Broiler-fryers are young chickens weighing two to three pounds. They are only seven to ten weeks old and yield tender, mildly flavored meat. They are available whole, halved, quartered and cut into parts. Broiler-fryers are best when broiled, fried, grilled, roasted or sautéed.

Roasters are chickens that are about four months old and weigh three to eight pounds. They are most often available whole. As the name implies, they are perfect for roasting and rotisserie cooking.

Capons are young, castrated roosters weighing six to eight pounds. These richly flavored birds have a higher fat content and yield more meat than roasters.

Stewing chickens or hens are older birds that weigh from three to six pounds. They are tough but flavorful. They require a moist cooking method such as stewing. These birds are excellent for making soups and stocks.

Cut-up chickens are whole broiler-fryers that have been cut into parts, consisting of two breast halves, two thighs, two wings and two drumsticks. The backbone may or may not be cut away from the breasts. Some markets may divide chickens differently, sometimes with labels such as "choice cuts," which mean different things in different markets. Be sure to read the label carefully to make sure that you get what you want.

Chicken pieces are available in packages of just breasts, wings, thighs or drumsticks. Broiler-fryers are usually used for pieces.

Boneless, skinless chicken is a favorite choice for today's busy cook because of its convenience and quick-cooking appeal. Boneless breasts, sometimes called cutlets, plus chicken tenders and boneless thighs are available.

Shopping Tips

Once you have determined the kind of chicken you wish to buy, follow these important tips when purchasing chicken.

• Look for secure, unbroken packaging, as well as a "sell-by" date that indicates the last day the chicken should be sold.

• Inspect the chicken before purchasing. The skin should be creamy white to deep yellow; skin color is dependent on the chicken's diet. The chicken should be plump; the meat should never look gray or pasty.

• Odors signal spoilage. If you notice a strong, unpleasant odor after opening a package of chicken, return the chicken in its original packaging to the store for a refund.

• Save time by stocking the freezer with ready-to-use boneless, skinless chicken. Store the chicken in efficient meal-size portions.

• Two whole chicken breasts yield about two cups chopped cooked chicken; one broiler-fryer (about three pounds) yields about two and one-half cups chopped cooked chicken.

Storing

• Raw chicken is very perishable and must be handled with care. Buy it just before returning home and refrigerate it as soon as possible.

• Fresh raw chicken can be stored in its original packaging for up to two days in the coldest part of the refrigerator.

• Freeze chicken immediately if you do not plan to use it within two days after purchasing. You can freeze raw chicken, tightly wrapped in plastic wrap, freezer paper or foil, for up to one year.

• Cooked chicken can be frozen for up to two months.

• When freezing whole chickens, remove and rinse the giblets (if any) and pat dry with paper towels. Rinse and dry the chicken and trim away any excess fat. Tightly wrap, label, date and freeze chicken and giblets separately in plastic wrap, freezer paper or foil. Giblets should be used within two or three months.

• When freezing chicken pieces, consider wrapping them individually in plastic wrap. Overwrap several pieces or place them in a resealable freezer bag. This will allow you to remove and thaw only the amount you need. Individual pieces removed from the overwrap or freezer bag will also thaw more quickly.

• Airtight packaging is the key to freezing chicken successfully, because it prevents the formation of ice crystals.

• Thaw frozen chicken, wrapped, in the refrigerator for best results. Allow at least 24 hours thawing time for a 5-pound whole chicken. Allow five hours thawing time per pound of chicken pieces.

• **DO NOT** allow other food to come in contact with a thawing chicken or its juices.

Handling

Raw chicken can contain salmonella bacteria, but with careful handling and proper cooking methods you can eliminate any health concerns. Follow these helpful tips for safe handling of chicken.

• Raw chicken should be rinsed and patted dry with paper towels before cooking. Cutting boards and knives must be washed in hot sudsy water after using and before reusing for any other food preparation. Wash your hands thoroughly before and after handling raw chicken.

• **DO NOT** thaw frozen chicken on the kitchen counter, because bacteria grow more quickly at room temperature; thaw chicken in the refrigerator. Never refreeze chicken that has been thawed.

• Always cook chicken completely. **DO NOT** partially cook, then store it to be finished cooking later.

• When stuffing chicken, lightly stuff the cavity just before cooking. **DO NOT** stuff chicken ahead of time.

• Chicken should be eaten, refrigerated or frozen within two hours of cooking.

Is It Done Yet?

There are several ways to determine when chicken is completely cooked and therefore safe to eat.

Whole chickens: A meat thermometer inserted into the thickest part of the thigh, but not touching bone or fat, should register 180°F before removing the chicken from the oven.

Whole chickens, stuffed: A meat thermometer inserted into the center of the stuffing in the body cavity should register 165°F.

Whole chicken breasts: A meat thermometer inserted into the thickest part should register 170°F.

Bone-in chicken pieces: You should be able to insert a fork into chicken pieces with ease and the juices should run clear when they are completely cooked. However, the meat and juices nearest the bone might still be pink even though the chicken is completely cooked. The color is caused by hemoglobin, which is an iron-containing pigment located in red blood cells. The pinkish coloring is usually noticed in young chickens, which have less fat than more mature chickens.

Boneless chicken pieces: The center of the chicken piece should no longer be pink. To check, just cut into the chicken with a knife.

Helpful Preparation Techniques

Disjointing a Whole Chicken

Place chicken, breast side up, on a cutting board. Cut between the thigh and body to the hip joint. Bend the leg back slightly to free the hip joint from its socket; cut through the hip joint and remove the leg. Repeat to remove the other leg.

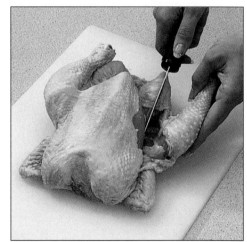

Place the leg, skin side down, on the cutting board. Locate the joint by moving the thigh back and forth with one hand while holding the drumstick with the other hand. Cut completely through the joint.

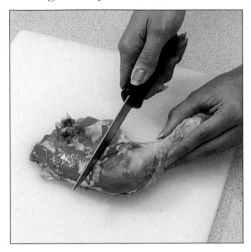

Place the chicken on its side. Pull one wing out from the body; cut through the shoulder joint. Turn chicken over and repeat to remove the other wing.

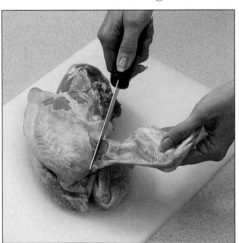

Working from the tail to the neck, cut the breast from the backbone, cutting through the small rib bones and along the outside of the collarbone.

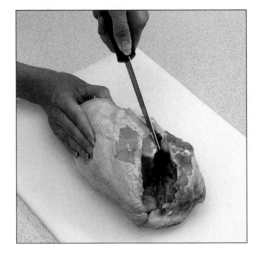

Turn the chicken over and repeat on the other side. Cut through any remaining connective tissue; pull the breast away from the backbone.

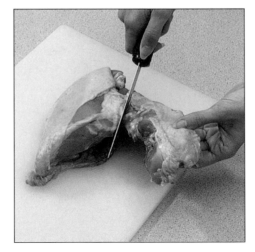

Place the breast, skin side up, on the cutting board. Split the breast into halves by cutting along one side of the breastbone. If desired, you may debone the whole breast before splitting (see Skinning and Deboning a Whole Chicken Breast, page 8).

Cutting a Whole Chicken into Halves and Quarters

Place the chicken, breast side down, on a cutting board with the neck end away from you. Working from the neck to the tail, cut along one side of the backbone, cutting as close to the bone as possible. Cut down the other side of the backbone; remove the backbone.

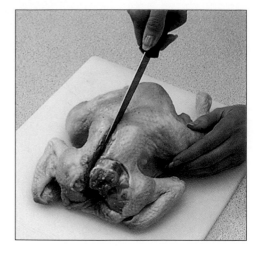

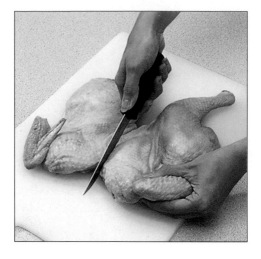

Remove the breastbone (see Skinning and Deboning a Whole Chicken Breast page 8).

To cut into quarters, cut through the skin that separates the thigh from the breast.

meat; discard skin. Be sure to launder the kitchen towel before using it again. For easier skin removal, freeze chicken pieces until firm but not hard before removing the skin. (However, do not refreeze thawed chicken.)

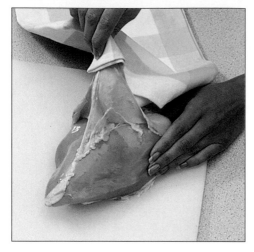

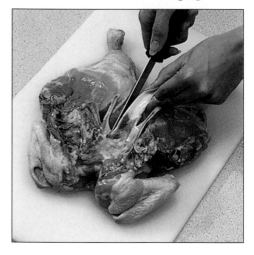

Turn the chicken skin side up. Cut lengthwise down the center of the chicken to split it into halves.

Skinning and Deboning a Whole Chicken Breast

Grasp the skin with a clean cotton kitchen towel or paper towel and pull away from the

Place the breast, meaty side down, on the cutting board with the widest part nearest you. Cut through the membrane and cartilage at the V of the neck end.

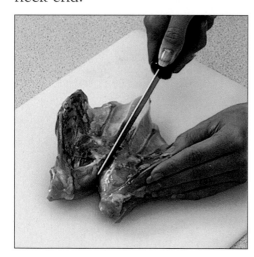

Grasp the breast with your hands and gently bend sides backward to snap the breastbone.

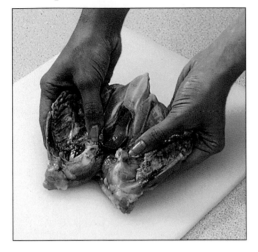

With the tip of a sharp knife, cut along the sides of the cartilage at the end of the breastbone. Remove cartilage.

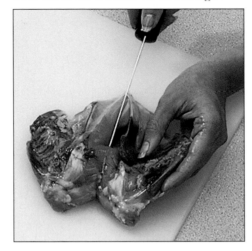

Cut meat away from the collarbone. Remove bones. Repeat procedure to debone the other side of the breast.

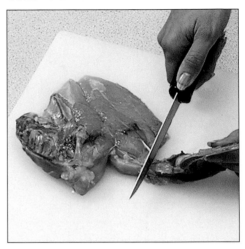

With your fingers, work along both sides of the breastbone to loosen the triangular keel bone; pull out the bone.

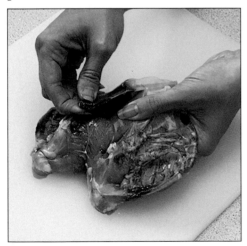

Slip the point of the knife under the long rib bones on one side of the breast. Cut and scrape meat from the rib bones, pulling the bones away from the meat.

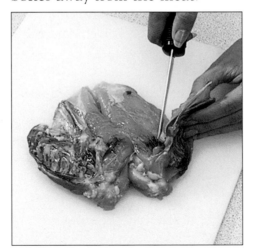

Remove the wishbones of chicken breasts that have been cut from whole chickens in your home kitchen. (The wishbones will already be removed from bone-in chicken breasts purchased from a supermarket or butcher.) Cut meat away from the wishbone at the neck end of the breast. Grasp the wishbone and pull it out of the breast.

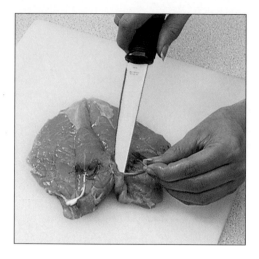

To remove the white tendon from each side of the breast, cut enough meat away from each tendon so you can grasp it (use a paper towel for firmer grasp). Remove tendon.

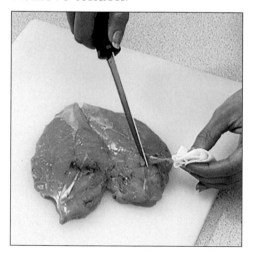

Trim any loosened remaining connective tissue or fat. Cut the whole chicken breast into halves lengthwise.

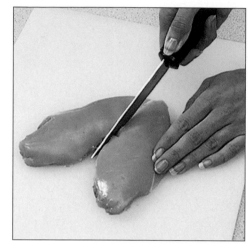

To remove chicken tenders, place breast, skinned side down, on cutting board. Grasp the tubular tender that runs the length of the outer edge of the breast half in one hand and the breast half in the other and pull apart.

Flattening Uncooked Boneless Chicken Breasts

Place one chicken breast half between two sheets of waxed paper. Using the flat side of a meat mallet or rolling pin, gently pound chicken to the desired thickness.

Shredding Cooked Chicken

Place cooked boneless chicken on a cutting board. Pull meat into long shreds with your fingers or two forks.

Cooking Methods

Sautéing is a quick-cooking method in which chicken pieces are browned in a small amount of vegetable oil or fat over medium or medium-high heat; the pieces are turned frequently. Thin cuts, such as boneless chicken breasts and cutlets, will be completely cooked during browning. For thicker pieces, reduce the heat, cover and cook gently until the chicken is no longer pink in the center. Sautéing promotes even cooking and produces a crisp, brown surface that locks in flavorful juices. It is an ideal way to cook boneless, skinless chicken breasts. It is also the first step in the braising method and in the preparation of chicken for some casseroles.

Pan-frying is a quick-cooking method in which chicken pieces are usually coated with seasoned flour or bread crumbs and cooked in a skillet in approximately one-half inch of hot vegetable oil or fat over medium to medium-high heat.

Deep-frying is similar to pan-frying except the chicken pieces, coated with seasoned flour or batter, are submerged in hot vegetable oil or fat for cooking.

Braising is a two-step cooking method in which chicken pieces are first browned in a small amount of vegetable oil or fat (sautéed), then slowly cooked, covered, in a small amount of liquid, such as water or broth, over low heat. During the slow-cooking stage, the chicken flavors combine with the other ingredients resulting in tender, tasty meat.

Poaching is the method of gently simmering chicken pieces in a liquid, such as water or broth. The amount and temperature of the liquid depends on the cut of chicken being poached. Meat from poached chicken is tender and juicy in texture and mild in flavor. Poached chicken meat is generally used for salads, casseroles, sandwiches or any recipe calling for cooked chicken.

Roasting is the dry heat method of cooking whole chicken, uncovered, in the oven; it results in a well-browned exterior and a moist and tender interior. To prepare a whole chicken for roasting, remove the giblets from the chicken cavity and discard them or reserve for another use. Rinse the chicken under cold water and pat dry with paper towels. Insert a meat thermometer into the center of the thickest part of the thigh, but not touching bone. Tuck the wings under the back and tie the legs together with wet cotton string. Place the chicken, breast side up, on a rack in a roasting pan. To prevent the chicken from drying out, baste with pan juices every 10 to 15 minutes. When the chicken has reached the proper temperature, remove it from the oven, loosely cover with foil and let it stand 10 to 15 minutes before carving.

Broiling is done by cooking chicken pieces four to six inches above or below the heat source as in an oven or on a range-top grill. The chicken is cooked on both sides until the outside is browned and the inside is moist and tender. Broiling can dry out chicken. To avoid this, marinate the chicken before broiling or brush the chicken with oil, butter or a flavorful sauce, such as barbecue sauce, during broiling.

Grilling is done by cooking chicken pieces, quarters or halves on a grill grid directly over hot coals. Make sure there is enough charcoal in a single layer to extend one to two inches beyond the area of the food on the grill.

Hearty
SOUPS, SALADS
& SANDWICHES

Basil, Chicken and Vegetables on Focaccia

½ cup mayonnaise
½ teaspoon black pepper, divided
¼ teaspoon garlic powder
1 loaf (16 ounces) focaccia or Italian bread, sliced
6 boneless skinless chicken breasts halves (about 2¼ pounds)
3 tablespoons olive oil
2 cloves garlic, minced
1½ teaspoons dried basil leaves
½ teaspoon salt
1 green bell pepper, cut into sixths
1 zucchini, cut lengthwise into 4 slices
3 Italian plum tomatoes, sliced

COMBINE mayonnaise, ¼ teaspoon black pepper and garlic powder in small bowl; set aside.

CUT focaccia into 6 pieces. Cut each piece horizontally in half; set aside.

COMBINE chicken, oil, garlic, basil, salt and remaining ¼ teaspoon black pepper in large resealable plastic food storage bag. Seal bag; turn to coat. Add bell pepper and zucchini; turn to coat.

GRILL or broil chicken, bell pepper and zucchini 4 inches from heat source 6 to 8 minutes on each side or until chicken is no longer pink in center. (Bell pepper and zucchini may take less time.)

TOP half of each focaccia piece with mayonnaise mixture, tomatoes, bell pepper, zucchini and chicken. Top with focaccia tops.

Makes 6 servings

Basil, Chicken and Vegetables on Focaccia

Gazebo Chicken

4 boneless chicken breast halves (about
    1½ pounds)
6 cups torn butter lettuce leaves or mixed
    baby greens
1 ripe cantaloupe, seeded and cut into
    12 wedges
1 large carrot, shredded
½ cup (3 ounces) fresh raspberries
⅔ cup honey-mustard salad dressing, divided

1. Preheat broiler. Place chicken, skin side down, on broiler pan coated with nonstick cooking spray. Season with salt and pepper to taste. Broil 4 to 5 inches from heat source 8 minutes. Turn; sprinkle with salt and pepper. Broil 6 to 8 minutes or until chicken is no longer pink in center. Remove to cutting board; cool.

2. Place lettuce on large serving platter; arrange cantaloupe and carrot around lettuce.

3. Slice each chicken breast diagonally into fourths; place over lettuce.

4. Arrange raspberries over salad; drizzle with 2 tablespoons dressing. Serve with remaining dressing. *Makes 4 servings*

Prep and cook time: 25 minutes

Serving Suggestion: Serve salad with corn muffins and herb-flavored butter.

Mandarin Chicken Salad

1 whole chicken breast, split
2 cups water
4 tablespoons KIKKOMAN® Soy Sauce,
    divided
  Boiling water
¾ pound fresh bean sprouts
1 carrot, peeled and shredded
½ cup slivered green onions and tops
2 tablespoons minced fresh cilantro or
    parsley
¼ cup distilled white vinegar
2 teaspoons sugar
½ cup blanched slivered almonds, toasted

Simmer chicken in mixture of 2 cups water and 1 tablespoon soy sauce in covered saucepan 15 minutes, or until chicken is tender. Meanwhile, pour boiling water over bean sprouts. Drain; cool under cold water and drain thoroughly. Remove chicken and cool. (Refrigerate stock for another use, if desired.) Skin and bone chicken; shred meat with fingers into large bowl. Add bean sprouts, carrot, green onions and cilantro. Blend vinegar, remaining 3 tablespoons soy sauce and sugar, stirring until sugar dissolves. Pour over chicken and vegetables; toss to coat all ingredients. Cover and refrigerate 1 hour. Just before serving, add almonds and toss to combine.
Makes 4 to 6 servings

Gazebo Chicken

Hot and Sour Soup

3 cans (about 14 ounces each) chicken broth
½ pound boneless skinless chicken breasts, cut into ¼-inch-thick strips
1 cup shredded carrots
1 cup sliced mushrooms
½ cup bamboo shoots, cut into matchstick-size strips
2 tablespoons rice or white wine vinegar
½ to ¾ teaspoon white pepper
¼ to ½ teaspoon hot pepper sauce
2 tablespoons cornstarch
2 tablespoons soy sauce
1 tablespoon dry sherry
2 medium green onions, sliced
1 egg, slightly beaten

COMBINE chicken broth, chicken, carrots, mushrooms, bamboo shoots, vinegar, white pepper and pepper sauce in large saucepan; bring to a boil over medium-high heat. Reduce heat to low. Cover and simmer about 5 minutes or until chicken is no longer pink in center.

STIR together cornstarch, soy sauce and sherry in small bowl until smooth. Add to chicken broth mixture. Bring to a boil, stirring constantly. Stir in green onions. While stirring constantly in one direction, slowly pour egg into soup; cook about 1 minute, until egg is cooked. Ladle soup into bowls.   *Makes 6 servings*

Thai Chicken Sandwiches

2 boneless, skinless chicken breast halves
¼ cup prepared peanut sauce
4 slices (4 ounces) SARGENTO® Sliced Mozzarella Cheese
4 pita bread rounds, cut in halves
½ cup bean sprouts
½ cup shredded carrot
½ cup thin diagonally sliced green onions
¼ cup thinly sliced radishes *or* 1 small red bell pepper, cut into thin strips
Additional prepared peanut sauce

1. Slice chicken into 3-inch-long strips, about ¼ inch thick. Coat with peanut sauce. Cook on oiled grill over medium coals (coals will be ash gray) 2 minutes on each side or until no longer pink.

2. Cut each cheese slice into quarters. Soften pita according to package directions. Fill each pita pocket half with chicken, cheese, bean sprouts, carrot, green onions and radishes. Drizzle with additional peanut sauce, if desired.

Makes 4 servings

Prep time: 15 minutes

Grill time: 4 minutes

Variation: To broil, place chicken on broiler pan. Broil 4 inches from heat source, 2 minutes on each side or until no longer pink. Continue as directed.

Open-Faced Chicken Sandwiches with Broiled Vegetables

1 small red onion, cut into ¼-inch slices
1 package (8 ounces) sliced portobello
    mushrooms
1 cup Italian salad dressing
4 boneless skinless chicken breast halves
4 slices whole grain bread
4 leaves leaf lettuce
1 cup avocado, cut into ½-inch cubes
¼ cup bacon bits

1. Preheat broiler.

2. Dip onion and mushroom slices in Italian dressing; set aside.

3. Pound chicken breast halves between 2 pieces of plastic wrap to ½-inch thickness with flat side of meat mallet or rolling pin. Dip chicken in remaining Italian dressing.

4. Place chicken on broiler pan; broil 4 to 5 inches from heat source 4 minutes per side or until no longer pink in center. Broil onion and mushrooms with chicken during last 4 minutes of cooking time.

5. Top bread slices with lettuce leaves, chicken, mushrooms, onion, avocado and bacon bits.

Makes 4 servings

Prep and cook time: 20 minutes

Variation: Place 1 slice Monterey Jack cheese on top of avocado and return sandwich to broiler until cheese is melted. Sprinkle with bacon bits.

Oriental Chicken Cabbage

SALAD

4 cups green and red shredded cabbage
2 cups chopped cooked chicken
1 cup blanched snow peas
½ cup shredded carrot
½ cup sliced green onions
1 (8-ounce) can sliced water chestnuts,
    drained
1 (3-ounce) package dry oriental noodle
    soup mix
2 tablespoons toasted sesame seeds
1 cup large pieces DIAMOND® Walnuts

ORIENTAL DRESSING

¼ cup oil
¼ cup seasoned rice vinegar
2 tablespoons sugar
1 tablespoon soy sauce
1 clove garlic, minced
½ teaspoon grated gingerroot

In large serving bowl, combine cabbage, chicken, snow peas, carrot, onions and water chestnuts. Combine all dressing ingredients; blend well. Pour dressing over salad; toss well. Break noodles into bite-size pieces (reserve dry seasoning packet for another use). Add noodles, sesame seeds and walnuts to salad; toss and serve.

Makes 6 to 8 servings

*Open-Faced Chicken Sandwich
with Broiled Vegetables*

Easy Oriental Chicken Sandwiches

¼ cup peanut butter
2 tablespoons honey
2 tablespoons reduced-sodium soy sauce
½ teaspoon garlic powder
½ teaspoon ground ginger
¼ teaspoon ground red pepper
4 boneless skinless chicken breasts halves
    (about 1½ pounds)
4 onion or kaiser rolls, split
    Lettuce leaves
1 cup sliced cucumbers
1 cup bean sprouts
¼ cup sliced green onions

PREHEAT oven to 400°F. Combine peanut butter, honey, soy sauce, garlic powder, ginger and red pepper in small bowl; stir until well blended. Reserve ¼ cup peanut sauce.

PLACE chicken on foil-lined baking sheet. Spread remaining peanut sauce over chicken. Bake 20 minutes or until chicken is no longer pink in center.

FILL rolls with lettuce, cucumbers, bean sprouts and chicken; sprinkle with green onions. Serve with reserved peanut sauce.   *Makes 4 servings*

Chicken Salad Primavera in Pita

3 cups diced cooked chicken thighs
    (1 pound)
1½ cups broccoli flowerettes, blanched
1½ cups sliced carrots, blanched
¾ cup chopped red bell pepper
⅔ cup mayonnaise
⅓ cup GREY POUPON® COUNTRY
    DIJON® Mustard
1 tablespoon red wine vinegar
¼ teaspoon dried tarragon leaves
    Lettuce leaves
6 (5-inch) whole wheat pita breads, split
    Alfalfa sprouts, optional

In large bowl, combine chicken, broccoli, carrots and bell pepper; set aside. In small bowl, combine mayonnaise, mustard, vinegar and tarragon. Add to chicken mixture; stir to coat. Cover; chill at least 1 hour.

Serve chicken mixture in lettuce-lined pitas. If desired, top with alfalfa sprouts.

Makes 6 servings

Prep time: 20 minutes
Chill time: 1 hour

Easy Oriental Chicken Sandwich

Southwest White Chili

SPICE BLEND

1 teaspoon MCCORMICK®/SCHILLING® California Style Garlic Powder
1 teaspoon MCCORMICK®/SCHILLING® Ground Cumin
½ teaspoon MCCORMICK®/SCHILLING® Oregano Leaves
½ teaspoon MCCORMICK®/SCHILLING® Cilantro Leaves
⅛ to ¼ teaspoon MCCORMICK®/SCHILLING® Ground Red Pepper

CHILI

1 tablespoon olive oil
1 pound boneless, skinless chicken breasts, cut into ½-inch cubes
¼ cup chopped onion
1 cup chicken broth
1 can (4 ounces) chopped green chilies, undrained
1 can (19 ounces) white kidney beans (cannellini), undrained
Shredded Monterey Jack cheese
Sliced scallions, for garnish

1. Place all ingredients for spice blend in small dish and stir until well blended. Set aside.

2. Heat oil in 2- to 3-quart saucepan over medium-high heat. Add chicken; cook and stir 4 to 5 minutes. Remove chicken with slotted spoon; cover and keep warm.

3. Add onion to saucepan; cook and stir 2 minutes. Stir in chicken broth, chilies and spice blend. Simmer over low heat 20 minutes.

4. Stir in beans and chicken; simmer, uncovered, 10 minutes.

5. Spoon into serving dish and sprinkle with cheese and scallions.   *Makes 4 servings*

Caesar Chicken Sandwiches

3 tablespoons all-purpose flour
½ teaspoon ground black pepper
4 boneless skinless chicken breast halves
Vegetable oil cooking spray
6 tablespoons lemon juice
4 cloves garlic, minced
4 teaspoons Worcestershire sauce
Dash hot pepper sauce
2 tablespoons PLANTERS® Gold Measure Walnuts, toasted and chopped
4 teaspoons grated Parmesan cheese
4 romaine lettuce leaves
4 whole wheat sandwich rolls, sliced lengthwise

Combine flour and pepper. Coat chicken with flour mixture, shaking off excess. Spray a 10-inch skillet with cooking spray for 2 seconds; over medium heat, lightly brown chicken on both sides. Combine lemon juice, garlic, Worcestershire and pepper sauce; pour over chicken. Cover; simmer for 15 minutes or until chicken is done. Sprinkle walnuts and cheese over chicken. Arrange lettuce on rolls; top with chicken. Serve immediately.

Makes 4 sandwiches

Chicken and Andouille Gumbo

½ pound andouille or kielbasa sausage, cut
    into ¼-inch cubes
4 tablespoons vegetable oil, divided
1 2½- to 3-pound chicken, cut into pieces
1½ quarts water
⅓ cup all-purpose flour
1 cup chopped onion
1 cup chopped celery
1 cup chopped green bell pepper
2 cloves garlic, minced
2 tablespoons chopped fresh parsley
2 bay leaves
½ teaspoon dried thyme
1 teaspoon TABASCO® pepper sauce
¼ teaspoon salt
⅛ teaspoon freshly ground black pepper
½ cup chopped green onions
    Cooked rice

In 3-quart saucepan, over medium-high heat, brown sausage in 2 tablespoons oil, about 7 minutes. Remove with slotted spoon and set aside. Add chicken pieces and cook until golden brown, about 10 minutes, turning occasionally. Add water; cover and cook until chicken is tender, about 30 minutes. Remove chicken, leaving liquid in pan; when chicken is cool enough to handle, discard skin and bones and dice meat into ½-inch cubes.

In skillet, over medium heat, mix remaining 2 tablespoons oil and flour and cook, stirring constantly, until roux turns dark brown, about 30 minutes. Add onion, celery, bell pepper, garlic and parsley and cook about 10 minutes or until vegetables are tender. Add vegetable mixture to liquid in saucepan along with bay leaves, thyme, TABASCO® sauce, salt and black pepper. Bring to a boil. Reduce heat and simmer, uncovered, 45 minutes. Add chicken and sausage; simmer another 15 minutes.

Remove pan from heat, add green onions and adjust seasoning, if necessary. Let gumbo stand 10 to 15 minutes. To serve, mound about ⅓ cup rice in each soup bowl, then ladle about 1 cup gumbo around rice. *Makes 8 servings*

Southwestern Chicken Soup

4 cups chicken broth
½ cup long-grain rice, uncooked
¼ teaspoon ground cumin
1 cup chopped cooked chicken
½ cup fresh corn kernels (frozen corn
    kernels may be substituted)
2 tablespoons SONOMA Dried Tomato Bits®
¼ cup fresh lime juice
¼ teaspoon cayenne pepper
    Salt, to taste

In large saucepan, bring chicken broth to a boil. Stir in rice and cumin. Cover and cook 15 minutes or until rice is done. Stir in chicken and corn. Cover and bring just to a boil; remove from heat. Stir in tomato bits, lime juice, cayenne and salt. *Makes 4 servings*

Mandarin Chicken Salad

1 cup rice-flour noodles
1 can (6 ounces) mandarin orange segments,
    chilled
⅓ cup honey
2 tablespoons rice vinegar
2 tablespoons reduced-sodium soy sauce
1 can (8 ounces) sliced water chestnuts,
    drained
4 cups shredded napa cabbage
1 cup shredded red cabbage
½ cup sliced radishes
4 thin slices red onion, cut in half and
    separated
3 boneless skinless chicken breast halves
    (about 12 ounces), cooked, cooled and
    cut into strips

1. Place rice-flour noodles in medium bowl; cover with water. Let stand 10 minutes; drain. Drain mandarin orange segments, reserving ⅓ cup liquid. Whisk together reserved liquid, honey, vinegar and soy sauce in small bowl. Add water chestnuts.

2. Divide napa and red cabbages, radishes and onion evenly among four serving plates. Top with chicken and orange segments. Remove water chestnuts from dressing and arrange on salads. Serve with rice-flour noodles; drizzle with remaining dressing.   *Makes 4 servings*

Prep and cook time: 20 minutes

Chicken-Barley Soup

3 tablespoons butter
1 large onion, chopped
2 cloves garlic, minced or pressed
6 cups chicken broth
¼ cup pearl barley, uncooked
¼ teaspoon dried thyme leaves
2 large carrots, thinly sliced
2 cups cubed cooked chicken
3 tablespoons SONOMA Dried Tomato Bits®
    Salt and freshly ground pepper, to taste
4 sprigs fresh cilantro for garnish, optional

Melt butter over medium heat in 3- to 4-quart pan. Add onion and garlic; cook until onion is soft, stirring occasionally, about 10 minutes. Add chicken broth, barley and thyme. Bring to a boil over high heat. Reduce heat; cover and simmer until barley is tender, about 30 minutes. Add carrots; simmer, covered, until carrots are tender when pierced with a fork, about 10 minutes. Add chicken and tomato bits; cook until heated through, about 5 minutes. Season with salt and pepper; serve in bowls. Garnish with cilantro, if desired.   *Makes 4 servings*

Mandarin Chicken Salad

Chicken and Vegetable Chowder

1 pound boneless skinless chicken breasts, cut into 1-inch pieces
10 ounces frozen broccoli cuts
1 cup sliced carrots
½ cup chopped onion
½ cup frozen corn
1 jar (4½ ounces) sliced mushrooms, drained
2 cloves garlic, minced
½ teaspoon dried thyme leaves
1 can (about 14 ounces) reduced-sodium chicken broth
1 can (10¾ ounces) condensed cream of potato soup
⅓ cup half-and-half

COMBINE all ingredients except half-and-half in slow cooker. Cover and cook on LOW 5 hours or until vegetables are tender and chicken is no longer pink in center. Stir in half-and-half. Turn to HIGH. Cover and cook 15 minutes or until heated through.   *Makes 6 servings*

Variation: If desired, ½ cup (2 ounces) shredded Swiss or Cheddar cheese can be added just before serving, stirring over LOW heat until melted.

Warm Chicken and Rice Salad

¾ pound sliced boneless chicken breast
½ cup chopped pecans
1 tablespoon butter or margarine
1⅓ cups water
1 package (4 ounces) FARMHOUSE® Long Grain & Wild Rice
1 cup broccoli flowerets
½ cup julienned red bell pepper
¼ cup sliced scallions

VINAIGRETTE
¼ cup vegetable oil
2 tablespoons white wine vinegar
2 tablespoons orange juice
1 teaspoon orange peel
1 teaspoon honey
¼ teaspoon salt
⅛ teaspoon ground black pepper

In large skillet, sauté chicken and pecans in butter until chicken is no longer pink. Add water; bring to a boil. Add rice and contents of seasoning packet, reduce heat to low; cover and cook 10 minutes. Add broccoli, cook 10 minutes longer or until liquid is absorbed.

To prepare vinaigrette, in blender container, combine all vinaigrette ingredients. Blend on high speed 1 minute; set aside. In large bowl, combine rice mixture with bell pepper and scallions. Toss with vinaigrette. Serve warm.
          Makes 4 servings

Chicken and Vegetable Chowder

Spicy Chicken Salad in Peanut Sauce

⅔ cup chicken broth
2 tablespoons soy sauce
2 cloves garlic, crushed
½ to 1 teaspoon hot pepper sauce
⅓ cup creamy peanut butter
2 teaspoons dark sesame oil
2 cups loosely packed fresh spinach, rinsed
    and patted dry
8 ounces linguine, cooked and drained
2 cups shredded cooked chicken
1 cup shredded carrots
¼ cup sliced green onions

COMBINE chicken broth, soy sauce, garlic and pepper sauce in medium saucepan; bring to a boil over medium heat. Remove from heat. Whisk in peanut butter and sesame oil until smooth.

ARRANGE spinach on 4 plates. Toss linguine with 3 tablespoons peanut sauce; spoon over spinach.

ADD chicken, carrots and green onions to remaining peanut sauce. Spoon over linguine.

Makes 4 servings

San Francisco Grilled Chicken Sandwiches

2 boneless, skinless chicken breast halves
3 tablespoons Italian or ranch salad dressing
2 slices (2 ounces) SARGENTO® Sliced
    Muenster or Swiss Cheese
2 kaiser rolls, split *or* 4 slices sourdough
    bread
8 spinach leaves
½ cup alfalfa sprouts
6 avocado slices
2 tablespoons thick salsa

Pound chicken breast halves to ¼-inch thickness. Place in shallow bowl; pour dressing over chicken. Cover; marinate in refrigerator 1 hour. Drain chicken; discard dressing. Grill chicken over medium coals 3 minutes; turn. Top each chicken breast half with Muenster cheese slice; continue to grill 2 to 3 minutes or until chicken is no longer pink. On bottom half of each roll layer *half* of the spinach leaves, sprouts and avocado slices. Top each sandwich with grilled chicken breast, half of salsa and top half of roll.

Makes 2 sandwiches

Spicy Chicken Salad in Peanut Sauce

Country Chicken Chowder

1 pound chicken tenders
2 tablespoons margarine or butter
1 small onion, chopped
1 rib celery, sliced
1 small carrot, sliced
1 can (10¾ ounces) cream of potato soup
1 cup milk
1 cup frozen corn
½ teaspoon dried dill weed

1. Cut chicken tenders into ½-inch pieces.

2. Melt margarine in large saucepan or Dutch oven over medium-high heat. Add chicken; cook and stir 5 minutes.

3. Add onion, celery and carrot; cook and stir 3 minutes. Stir in soup, milk, corn and dill; reduce heat to low. Cook about 8 minutes or until corn is tender and chowder is heated through. Add salt and pepper to taste.   *Makes 4 servings*

Prep and cook time: 27 minutes

For a special touch, garnish soup with croutons and fresh dill.

Summer Caesar Salad

Caesar Dressing (recipe follows)
2 tablespoons lemon juice
5 cloves garlic, pressed and divided
2 teaspoons dried rosemary
  Salt and black pepper
4 skinless boneless chicken breast halves
  (about 4 ounces each)
2 tablespoons olive oil
20 slices French bread baguette (about
  ¼ inch thick)
1 bag (10 ounces) romaine lettuce leaves *or*
  6 cups torn romaine lettuce leaves
Shaved Parmesan cheese

Prepare Caesar Dressing. Combine lemon juice, 4 cloves garlic, rosemary, and salt and pepper to taste; rub garlic mixture onto chicken. Combine oil and remaining 1 clove garlic in small cup; brush onto both sides of bread slices. Lightly oil grid to prevent sticking. Grill chicken on covered grill over medium-hot KINGSFORD® Briquets 8 to 10 minutes until chicken is no longer pink in center, turning once. Arrange bread slices around edge of grid. Grill until lightly toasted. Arrange lettuce on 4 plates. Slice chicken breasts; arrange chicken and bread over lettuce. Sprinkle with cheese. Serve with Caesar Dressing.

Makes 5 servings

Caesar Dressing: Whisk together ⅓ cup olive oil, 3 tablespoons lemon juice, 2 teaspoons grainy mustard, 2 teaspoons anchovy paste, 2 minced cloves garlic and ¼ teaspoon *each* Worcestershire sauce and black pepper.

Country Chicken Chowder

Mediterranean Chicken Salad Sandwiches

4 boneless skinless chicken breast halves
   (about 1½ pounds)
1 teaspoon dried basil leaves
¼ teaspoon salt
¼ teaspoon black pepper
1 cup chopped cucumber
½ cup mayonnaise
¼ cup chopped roasted red pepper
¼ cup pitted ripe olive slices
¼ cup plain yogurt
¼ teaspoon garlic powder
6 kaiser rolls, split
   Additional mayonnaise
   Lettuce leaves

PLACE chicken, ½ cup water, basil, salt and pepper in medium saucepan; bring to a boil. Reduce heat; simmer covered 10 to 12 minutes or until chicken is no longer pink in center. Remove chicken from saucepan; cool. Cut into ½-inch pieces.

COMBINE chicken, cucumber, mayonnaise, red pepper, olives, yogurt and garlic powder in medium bowl; toss to coat well.

SPREAD rolls with additional mayonnaise. Top with lettuce and chicken salad mixture.

Makes 6 servings

Warm Chicken Taco Salad

½ cup MIRACLE WHIP® or MIRACLE
   WHIP LIGHT® Salad Dressing, divided
4 boneless skinless chicken breast halves
   (about 1¼ pounds), cut into thin strips
1 cup chopped tomato
1 package (1¼ ounces) taco seasoning mix
4 cups tortilla chips
4 cups shredded lettuce
   KRAFT® Natural Shredded Sharp
      Cheddar Cheese
   Sliced pitted ripe olives
   Sliced green onion

HEAT 2 tablespoons of the dressing in large skillet on medium-high heat. Add chicken; cook and stir 5 minutes. Reduce heat to medium; stir in remaining dressing, tomato and seasoning mix.

COOK and stir 5 minutes or until thoroughly heated and chicken is cooked through.

LAYER chips, lettuce and chicken mixture on large platter. Top with cheese, olives and onion.

Makes 4 servings

Mediterranean Chicken Salad Sandwich

Sizzling
STIR-FRY MEALS

Chicken with Walnuts

   1 cup uncooked instant rice
   ½ cup chicken broth
   ¼ cup Chinese plum sauce
   2 tablespoons soy sauce
   2 teaspoons cornstarch
   2 tablespoons vegetable oil, divided
   3 cups frozen bell peppers and onions
   1 pound boneless skinless chicken breasts,
        cut into ¼-inch slices
   1 clove garlic, minced
   1 cup walnut halves

1. Cook rice according to package directions. Set aside.

2. Combine broth, plum sauce, soy sauce and cornstarch; set aside.

3. Heat 1 tablespoon oil in wok or large skillet over medium-high heat until hot. Add frozen peppers and onions; stir-fry 3 minutes or until crisp-tender. Remove vegetables from wok. Drain; discard liquid.

4. Heat remaining 1 tablespoon oil in wok until hot. Add chicken and garlic; stir-fry 3 minutes or until chicken is no longer pink.

5. Stir broth mixture; add to wok. Cook and stir 1 minute or until sauce thickens. Stir in vegetables and walnuts; cook 1 minute more. Serve with rice.   *Makes 4 servings*

Prep and cook time: 19 minutes

Chicken with Walnuts

Chicken and Vegetables with Mustard Sauce

    1 pound boneless skinless chicken breast
       halves
    1 tablespoon sugar
    2 teaspoons cornstarch
    2 teaspoons dry mustard
    3 tablespoons reduced-sodium soy sauce
    2 tablespoons water
    2 tablespoons rice vinegar
    2 tablespoons vegetable oil, divided
    2 cloves garlic, minced
    1 small red bell pepper, cut into short thin
       strips
    ½ cup thinly sliced celery
    1 small onion, cut into thin wedges
       Hot cooked Chinese egg noodles
       Fresh chives and yellow bell pepper rose
          for garnish

• Rinse chicken and pat dry with paper towels. Cut chicken into 1-inch pieces; set aside.

• Combine sugar, cornstarch and mustard in small bowl. Stir soy sauce, water and vinegar into cornstarch mixture until smooth; set aside.

• Heat wok over medium-high heat until hot. Drizzle 1 tablespoon oil into wok and heat 30 seconds. Add chicken and garlic; stir-fry 4 to 5 minutes or until chicken is no longer pink in center. Remove chicken to large bowl.

• Drizzle remaining 1 tablespoon oil into wok and heat 30 seconds. Add bell pepper, celery and onion; stir-fry 3 minutes or until vegetables are crisp-tender.

• Stir soy sauce mixture; add to wok. Stir-fry 30 seconds or until sauce boils and thickens.

• Return chicken and any accumulated juices to wok; cook until heated through. Serve with noodles. Garnish, if desired.   *Makes 4 servings*

Chicken Fried Rice

    1 bag SUCCESS® Rice
    ½ pound boneless skinless chicken, cut into
       ½-inch pieces
    ½ teaspoon salt
    ¼ teaspoon pepper
    2 tablespoons vegetable oil
    1 clove garlic, minced
    ½ teaspoon grated fresh ginger
    2 cups diagonally sliced green onions
    1 cup sliced fresh mushrooms
    2 tablespoons reduced-sodium soy sauce
    1 teaspoon sherry
    1 teaspoon Asian-style hot chili sesame oil
       (optional)

Prepare rice according to package directions.

Sprinkle chicken with salt and pepper; set aside. Heat oil in large skillet over medium-high heat. Add garlic and ginger; cook and stir 1 minute. Add chicken; stir-fry until no longer pink in center. Add green onions and mushrooms; stir-fry until tender. Stir in soy sauce, sherry and sesame oil. Add rice; heat thoroughly, stirring occasionally.   *Makes 6 servings*

Chicken and Vegetables with Mustard Sauce

Creamy Herbed Chicken

1 package (9 ounces) fresh or dried bow-tie
    pasta or fusilli
1 tablespoon vegetable oil
2 boneless skinless chicken breasts, halved
    (about 1 pound) and cut into ½-inch
    strips
1 small red onion, cut into slices
1 package (10 ounces) frozen green peas,
    thawed and drained
1 yellow or red bell pepper, cut into strips
½ cup chicken broth
1 container (8 ounces) soft cream cheese
    with garlic and herbs
  Salt
  Black pepper

1. Cook pasta in lightly salted boiling water according to package directions; drain.

2. Meanwhile, heat oil in large skillet or wok over medium-high heat. Add chicken and onion; stir-fry 3 minutes or until chicken is no longer pink. Add peas and bell pepper; stir-fry 4 minutes. Reduce heat to medium.

3. Stir in broth and cream cheese. Cook, stirring constantly, until cream cheese is melted. Combine pasta and chicken mixture in serving bowl; mix lightly. Season with salt and black pepper to taste. Garnish as desired.

Makes 4 servings

Chicken & Cabbage Stir-Fry

1 boneless, skinless chicken breast half
5 tablespoons KIKKOMAN® Stir-Fry Sauce,
    divided
2 tablespoons water
1 medium-size head green cabbage
3 tablespoons vegetable oil, divided
1 teaspoon minced fresh gingerroot
1 large carrot, cut into julienne strips
1 medium onion, chunked
2 ounces fresh snow peas, trimmed and cut
    diagonally into halves

Cut chicken into 1-inch pieces; coat with 1 tablespoon stir-fry sauce in small bowl. Combine remaining 4 tablespoons stir-fry sauce and water in small bowl; set aside. Cut enough cabbage into 1-inch chunks to measure 6 cups. Heat 1 tablespoon oil in hot wok or large skillet over medium-high heat. Add chicken and ginger and stir-fry 3 minutes; remove. Heat remaining 2 tablespoons oil in same pan. Add cabbage, carrot, onion and snow peas; stir-fry 6 minutes longer. Add chicken and stir-fry sauce mixture; cook and stir only until chicken and vegetables are coated with sauce and heated through.

Makes 4 servings

Chicken Stir-Fry

4 boneless, skinless chicken breast halves
(about 1½ pounds)
2 tablespoons vegetable oil
1 tablespoon cornstarch
2 tablespoons light soy sauce
2 tablespoons orange juice
1 bag (16 ounces) BIRDS EYE® frozen
Farm Fresh Mixtures Broccoli, Carrots
& Water Chestnuts

• Cut chicken into ½-inch-thick long strips.

• In wok or large skillet, heat oil over medium-high heat.

• Add chicken; cook 5 minutes, stirring occasionally.

• Meanwhile, in small bowl, combine cornstarch, soy sauce and orange juice; blend well and set aside.

• Add vegetables to chicken; cook 5 minutes more or until chicken is no longer pink in center, stirring occasionally.

• Stir in soy sauce mixture; cook 1 minute or until heated through.   *Makes 4 servings*

Prep time: 5 minutes

Cook time: 12 minutes

Serving Suggestion: Serve over hot cooked rice.

Kung Pao Chicken

1 pound boneless, skinless chicken
5 tablespoons KIKKOMAN® Stir-Fry Sauce,
divided
1 teaspoon vinegar
½ to ¾ teaspoon crushed red pepper
¼ teaspoon cornstarch
2 tablespoons water
3 tablespoons vegetable oil, divided
1 large clove garlic, minced
1 large onion, chunked
2 small green bell peppers, chunked
⅔ cup unsalted roasted peanuts

Cut chicken into 1-inch-square pieces; coat with 1 tablespoon stir-fry sauce in small bowl. Let stand 30 minutes. Meanwhile, combine remaining 4 tablespoons stir-fry sauce, vinegar and crushed red pepper in small bowl; set aside. Dissolve cornstarch in water in small bowl; set aside. Heat 1 tablespoon oil in hot wok or large skillet over high heat. Add chicken and garlic and stir-fry 3 minutes; remove. Heat remaining 2 tablespoons oil in same pan. Add onion; stir-fry 1 minute. Add bell peppers; stir-fry 4 minutes longer. Add chicken, stir-fry sauce mixture, cornstarch mixture and peanuts; cook and stir until sauce boils and thickens. Serve immediately.   *Makes 4 servings*

Sweet & Sour Cashew Chicken

1 can (16 ounces) cling peach slices in syrup
1 cup KIKKOMAN® Sweet & Sour Sauce
2 boneless, skinless chicken breast halves
1 tablespoon cornstarch
1 tablespoon KIKKOMAN® Soy Sauce
1 tablespoon minced fresh gingerroot
½ teaspoon sugar
2 tablespoons vegetable oil, divided
1 onion, chunked
1 green bell pepper, chunked
1 small carrot, cut diagonally into thin slices
⅓ cup roasted cashews

Reserving ⅓ cup syrup, drain peaches; cut slices in half. Blend reserved syrup and sweet & sour sauce; set aside. Cut chicken into 1-inch-square pieces. Combine cornstarch, soy sauce, ginger and sugar in medium bowl; stir in chicken. Heat 1 tablespoon oil in hot wok or large skillet over high heat. Add chicken and stir-fry 4 minutes; remove. Heat remaining 1 tablespoon oil in same pan. Add onion, bell pepper and carrot; stir-fry 4 minutes. Stir in chicken, sweet & sour sauce mixture, peaches and cashews; heat through. Serve immediately.   *Makes 4 servings*

Honey Nut Stir-Fry

1 pound boneless chicken breasts
¾ cup orange juice
⅓ cup honey
3 tablespoons soy sauce
1 tablespoon cornstarch
¼ teaspoon ground ginger
2 tablespoons vegetable oil, divided
2 large carrots, sliced diagonally
2 stalks celery, sliced diagonally
½ cup cashews or peanuts
  Hot cooked rice

Cut chicken into thin strips; set aside. Combine orange juice, honey, soy sauce, cornstarch and ginger in small bowl; mix well. Heat 1 tablespoon oil in large skillet over medium-high heat. Add carrots and celery; stir-fry about 3 minutes. Remove vegetables; set aside. Pour remaining 1 tablespoon oil into skillet. Add chicken; stir-fry about 3 minutes. Return vegetables to skillet; add sauce mixture and nuts. Cook and stir over medium-high heat until sauce comes to a boil and thickens. Serve over rice.

Makes 4 to 6 servings

Favorite recipe from **National Honey Board**

Sweet & Sour Cashew Chicken

First Moon Chicken Stir-Fry

      2 tablespoons cornstarch, divided
      3 tablespoons KIKKOMAN® Soy Sauce,
            divided
   2½ teaspoons sugar, divided
      1 clove garlic, pressed
      2 boneless, skinless chicken breast halves,
            cut into 1-inch squares
   ¾ cup water
      1 teaspoon distilled white vinegar
   ½ pound fresh broccoli, trimmed
      2 tablespoons vegetable oil, divided
      1 medium onion, chunked
      1 small carrot, cut diagonally into thin slices
   ½ teaspoon crushed red pepper
   ¼ pound fresh snow peas, trimmed and cut
            diagonally into halves

Combine 1 tablespoon *each* cornstarch and soy
sauce with ½ teaspoon sugar and garlic in
medium bowl; stir in chicken. Let stand 15
minutes. Meanwhile, combine water, remaining
2 tablespoons soy sauce, 1 tablespoon cornstarch,
2 teaspoons sugar and vinegar in small bowl; set
aside. Remove flowerets from broccoli; cut into
bite-size pieces. Peel stalks; cut diagonally into
thin slices. Heat 1 tablespoon oil in hot wok or
large skillet over high heat. Add chicken and
stir-fry 3 minutes; remove. Heat remaining 1
tablespoon oil in same pan. Add broccoli, onion,
carrot and crushed red pepper; stir-fry 3 minutes.
Add snow peas; stir-fry 2 minutes longer. Add
chicken and soy sauce mixture; cook and stir
until sauce boils and thickens.

Makes 4 servings

Mexican Chicken Stir-Fry

      1 package (about 1¾ pounds) PERDUE®
            FIT 'N EASY® Fresh Skinless &
            Boneless Chicken Breast Tenderloins
      1 teaspoon chili powder
   ½ teaspoon ground cumin
   ¼ teaspoon dried oregano leaves
      2 tablespoons olive oil, divided
      2 scallions, chopped
      1 clove garlic, minced
      1 can (4 ounces) chopped mild green chilies
      1 can (19 ounces) black beans, rinsed and
            drained
      Hot cooked rice

In medium bowl, place tenders. Add chili
powder, cumin, oregano and 1 tablespoon olive
oil; toss well. Heat wok or large, nonstick skillet
over medium-high heat. When hot, coat with
remaining 1 tablespoon oil. Add tenders; stir-fry
4 to 5 minutes until barely cooked through. Add
scallions, garlic, chilies and beans. Stir-fry 2 to 3
minutes longer until heated through. Serve with
rice.   *Makes 4 servings*

Prep time: about 15 minutes

First Moon Chicken Stir-Fry

Lemon Cashew Chicken Stir-Fry

1 tablespoon peanut oil
1 pound chicken tenders, cut into 1½-inch pieces
½ cup sliced mushrooms
¼ cup sliced green onions
2 cloves garlic, minced
1 cup matchstick-size carrot strips
½ cup reduced-sodium chicken broth
1 to 2 tablespoons dry sherry
2 teaspoons sugar
½ teaspoon grated lemon peel
3 tablespoons lemon juice
1 tablespoon cornstarch
⅛ teaspoon white pepper
1 package (6 ounces) frozen snow peas, thawed
3 cups hot cooked rice
⅓ cup chopped cashews

HEAT oil in large skillet over medium-high heat until hot. Add chicken; cook and stir 7 to 8 minutes or until chicken is no longer pink in center.

ADD mushrooms, green onions and garlic; cook and stir 1 minute or until vegetables are tender. Add carrots, chicken broth, sherry, sugar and lemon peel; cook and stir 1 to 2 minutes more.

COMBINE lemon juice, cornstarch and pepper in small bowl; stir until smooth. Pour cornstarch mixture over chicken; cook and stir 1 to 2 minutes or until slightly thickened.

ADD snow peas; cook and stir 1 minute or until heated through. Serve over rice; sprinkle with cashews. *Makes 6 servings*

Southwestern Style Stir-Fry

1 pound chicken or beef, cut into strips
1 tablespoon vegetable oil
½ cup prepared salsa or taco sauce*
1 bag (16 ounces) BIRDS EYE® frozen Farm Fresh Mixtures Pepper Stir-Fry

*Or, substitute 1 package taco seasoning mix, prepared according to package directions.

• Brown chicken in oil in large skillet. Stir in salsa.

• Cover and simmer 1 minute. Stir in vegetables.

• Cover and cook 5 minutes or until vegetables are tender. *Makes 3 to 4 servings*

Prep time: 5 minutes

Cook time: 12 to 15 minutes

Serving Suggestion: Serve in taco shells, soft tortillas or over rice.

Lemon Cashew Chicken Stir-Fry

Sweet and Sour Chicken

    6 ounces boneless skinless chicken breast
      halves
    2 tablespoons rice vinegar
    2 tablespoons reduced-sodium soy sauce
    3 cloves garlic, minced
    ½ teaspoon minced fresh ginger
    ¼ teaspoon crushed red pepper
    3 green onions with tops
    1 large green bell pepper
    1 teaspoon vegetable oil
    1 tablespoon cornstarch
    ½ cup reduced-sodium chicken broth
    2 tablespoons apricot fruit spread
    1 can (11 ounces) mandarin orange
      segments
    2 cups hot cooked rice or Chinese egg
      noodles

• Rinse chicken and pat dry with paper towels. Cut chicken crosswise into ½-inch-wide strips. Combine vinegar, soy sauce, garlic, ginger and crushed red pepper in large bowl. Add chicken and toss to coat; marinate 15 minutes.

• Meanwhile, cut onions into 1-inch pieces. Remove stem and seeds from bell pepper. Cut into 1-inch squares. Set aside.

• Heat wok over medium heat 2 minutes or until hot. Drizzle oil into wok. Drain chicken, reserving marinade. Add chicken to wok; stir-fry 3 minutes or until chicken is no longer pink. Add onions and bell pepper; stir-fry 3 minutes or until vegetables are crisp-tender.

• Stir reserved marinade into cornstarch in cup until smooth. Stir broth, fruit spread and cornstarch mixture into wok; cook and stir 1 minute or until sauce comes to a boil. Boil 1 minute.

• Stir in orange segments; cook until heated through. Serve with rice.　*Makes 4 servings*

Thai Chicken with Basil

    2 tablespoons vegetable oil, divided
    1 teaspoon chile paste*
    1 pound chicken breasts, cut into cubes
    ¾ cup straw mushrooms
    ½ cup baby corn
    3 tablespoons fish sauce
    1 tablespoon sugar
    1 cup fresh basil leaves**

*If chile paste is not available, substitute crushed dried red chile pepper and 2 tablespoons minced garlic.

**If available, use holy basil.

Heat wok on medium heat; add 1 tablespoon oil. Add chile paste and stir-fry about 3 minutes or until fragrant. Add remaining 1 tablespoon oil. Increase heat to high. Add chicken and stir-fry until no longer pink. Add mushrooms and baby corn; mix well. Add fish sauce, sugar and basil leaves. Stir until sugar has dissolved and basil leaves have wilted. Garnish with chiles. Serve on lettuce leaves with hot cooked rice.

Makes 4 servings

Favorite recipe from **The Sugar Association**

Sweet and Sour Chicken

Cilantro-Lime Chicken

1 pound boneless skinless chicken breast
halves
2 small onions
1 or 2 small green or red jalapeño peppers
1 piece fresh ginger (1 inch long), peeled
1 large lime
2 tablespoons vegetable oil
2 tablespoons chopped fresh cilantro
2 tablespoons reduced-sodium soy sauce
1 to 2 teaspoons sugar
Hot cooked rice
Cilantro sprigs, lime zest and red jalapeño
pepper strips for garnish

• Rinse chicken; pat dry with paper towels. Cut each breast half into 6 pieces. Cut each onion into 8 wedges. Cut jalapeño crosswise into slices, removing seeds, if desired.* Cut ginger into thin slices.

• Remove 3 strips of peel from lime with vegetable peeler. Cut lime peel into very fine shreds. Juice lime; measure 2 tablespoons juice.

• Heat wok over medium-high heat 1 minute or until hot. Drizzle oil into wok and heat 30 seconds. Add chicken, jalapeño and ginger; stir-fry about 3 minutes or until chicken is no longer pink in center. Reduce heat to medium.

• Add onions; stir-fry 5 minutes. Add lime peel, lime juice and chopped cilantro; stir-fry 1 minute. Add soy sauce and sugar to taste; stir until hot. Serve with rice. Garnish, if desired.

Makes 4 servings

*Jalapeños can sting and irritate the skin; wear rubber gloves when handling jalapeños and do not touch eyes. Wash hands after handling jalapeños.

Szechuan Stir-Fry

1 tablespoon plus 1½ teaspoons peanut oil
½ teaspoon sesame oil (optional)
¼ to ½ teaspoon chile paste with garlic
(optional)
1 cup broccoli florets
1 cup red bell pepper pieces (cut into 1-inch
squares)
⅓ cup thinly sliced scallions
1 package (about 1 pound) PERDUE® Fresh
Hot & Spicy Chicken Wings
2 tablespoons soy sauce
Hot cooked rice

In wok or large skillet over medium-high heat, heat oils and chile paste. Add broccoli; stir-fry 2 minutes. Add bell pepper and scallions; cook 1 to 2 minutes longer, stirring constantly. Add wings and soy sauce. Stir-fry 2 minutes or until wings are heated through. Serve over rice.

Makes 4 to 6 servings

Cilantro-Lime Chicken

Homey
CASSEROLE FAVORITES

Roasted Chicken and Vegetables over Wild Rice

3½ pounds chicken pieces
¾ cup olive oil vinaigrette dressing, divided
1 tablespoon margarine or butter, melted
1 package (6 ounces) long grain and wild rice mix
1 can (13¾ ounces) reduced-sodium chicken broth
1 small eggplant, cut into 1-inch pieces
2 medium red potatoes, cut into 1-inch pieces
1 medium yellow squash, cut into 1-inch pieces
1 medium zucchini, cut into 1-inch pieces
1 medium red onion, cut into wedges
1 package (4 ounces) crumbled feta cheese with basil
Chopped fresh cilantro (optional)
Fresh thyme sprig (optional)

REMOVE skin from chicken; discard. Combine chicken and ½ cup dressing in large resealable plastic food storage bag. Seal bag and turn to coat. Refrigerate 30 minutes or overnight.

PREHEAT oven to 375°F. Coat bottom of 13×9-inch baking dish with margarine.

ADD rice and seasoning packet from rice mix to prepared dish; stir in broth. Combine eggplant, potatoes, squash, zucchini and onion in large bowl. Place on top of rice mixture.

REMOVE chicken from bag and place on top of vegetables; discard marinade. Pour remaining ¼ cup dressing over chicken.

BAKE, uncovered, 45 minutes. Remove from oven and sprinkle with cheese. Bake 5 to 10 minutes or until chicken is no longer pink in centers, juices run clear and cheese is melted. Sprinkle with cilantro, if desired. Garnish with thyme, if desired.   *Makes 4 to 6 servings*

Roasted Chicken and Vegetables over Wild Rice

Artichoke-Olive Chicken Bake

1½ cups uncooked rotini pasta
1 tablespoon olive oil
1 medium onion, chopped
½ green bell pepper, chopped
2 cups shredded cooked chicken
1 can (14½ ounces) diced tomatoes with
    Italian-style herbs, undrained
1 can (14 ounces) artichoke hearts, drained
    and quartered
1 can (6 ounces) sliced black olives, drained
1 teaspoon dried Italian seasoning
2 cups (8 ounces) shredded mozzarella
    cheese
Fresh basil sprig (optional)

PREHEAT oven to 350°F. Spray 13×9-inch baking dish with nonstick cooking spray.

COOK pasta according to package directions until al dente. Drain and set aside.

Meanwhile, **HEAT** oil in large deep skillet over medium heat until hot. Add onion and bell pepper; cook and stir 1 minute. Add chicken, tomatoes with juice, pasta, artichokes, olives and Italian seasoning; mix until combined.

PLACE half of chicken mixture in prepared dish; sprinkle with half of cheese. Top with remaining chicken mixture and cheese.

BAKE, covered, 35 minutes or until hot and bubbly. Garnish with basil, if desired.

Makes 8 servings

Chicken Tetrazzini

8 ounces uncooked spaghetti, broken in half
3 tablespoons butter, divided
¼ cup all-purpose flour
1 teaspoon salt
½ teaspoon paprika
½ teaspoon celery salt
⅛ teaspoon pepper
2 cups milk
1 cup chicken broth
3 cups chopped cooked chicken
1 can (4 ounces) mushrooms, drained
¼ cup pimiento strips
¾ cup (3 ounces) grated Wisconsin
    Parmesan cheese, divided

In large saucepan, cook spaghetti according to package directions; drain. Return to same saucepan; add 1 tablespoon butter. Stir until melted. Set aside. In 3-quart saucepan, melt remaining 2 tablespoons butter over medium heat; stir in flour, salt, paprika, celery salt and pepper. Remove from heat; gradually stir in milk and chicken broth. Cook over medium heat, stirring constantly, until thickened. Add chicken, mushrooms, pimiento, spaghetti and ¼ cup cheese; heat thoroughly. Place chicken mixture on ovenproof platter or in shallow casserole; sprinkle remaining ½ cup cheese over top. Broil about 3 inches from heat until lightly browned.

Makes 6 to 8 servings

Favorite recipe from **Wisconsin Milk Marketing Board**

Artichoke-Olive Chicken Bake

Barbecue Chicken with Cornbread Topper

1½ pounds boneless skinless chicken breasts
　　and thighs
1 can (15 ounces) red beans, drained and
　　rinsed
1 can (8 ounces) tomato sauce
1 cup chopped green bell pepper
½ cup barbecue sauce
1 envelope (6.5 ounces) cornbread mix
　Ingredients for cornbread mix

1. Cut chicken into ¾-inch cubes. Heat nonstick skillet over medium heat. Add chicken; cook and stir 5 minutes or until no longer pink.

2. Combine chicken, beans, tomato sauce, bell pepper and barbecue sauce in 8-inch microwavable ovenproof dish. Cover and refrigerate up to 2 days.

3. To complete recipe, preheat oven to 375°F. Loosely cover chicken mixture with plastic wrap. Microwave at MEDIUM-HIGH (70% power) 8 minutes or until hot, stirring after 4 minutes.

4. While chicken mixture is heating, prepare cornbread mix according to package directions. Spoon batter over chicken mixture. Bake 15 to 18 minutes or until toothpick inserted in center of cornbread layer comes out clean.

Makes 8 servings

Note: This recipe can be prepared and served on the same day; omit chilling. Proceed to Step 3; microwave chicken mixture 6 minutes or until heated through, stirring after 3 minutes. Complete recipe as directed.

Spicy Chicken Tortilla Casserole

1 tablespoon vegetable oil
1 cup (1 small) chopped green bell pepper
1 cup (1 small) chopped onion
2 cloves garlic, finely chopped
1 pound (about 4) boneless, skinless chicken
　　breast halves, cut into bite-size pieces
2½ cups (24-ounce jar) ORTEGA® Thick &
　　Chunky Salsa, hot, medium or mild
½ cup (2¼-ounce can) sliced ripe olives
6 corn tortillas, cut into halves
2 cups (8 ounces) shredded Monterey Jack
　　or Cheddar cheese
　Sour cream (optional)

HEAT oil in large skillet over medium-high heat. Add bell pepper, onion and garlic; cook for 2 to 3 minutes or until vegetables are tender.

ADD chicken; cook, stirring frequently, for 3 to 5 minutes or until chicken is no longer pink in center. Stir in salsa and olives; remove from heat.

PLACE 6 tortilla halves onto bottom of 8-inch-square baking pan. Top with half of chicken mixture and 1 cup cheese; repeat. Bake, covered, in preheated 350°F. oven for 15 to 20 minutes or until bubbly. Serve with sour cream.

Makes 8 servings

Barbecue Chicken with Cornbread Topper

Quick Chicken Pot Pie

1 pound boneless skinless chicken thighs
1 can (about 14 ounces) chicken broth
3 tablespoons all-purpose flour
2 tablespoons butter, softened
1 package (10 ounces) frozen mixed
    vegetables, thawed
1 can (4 ounces) mushrooms, drained
¼ teaspoon dried basil leaves
¼ teaspoon dried oregano leaves
¼ teaspoon dried thyme leaves
1 cup biscuit baking mix
6 tablespoons milk

1. Cut chicken into 1-inch cubes. Place chicken and chicken broth in large skillet; cover and bring to a boil over high heat. Reduce heat to medium; simmer, uncovered, 5 minutes or until chicken is tender.

2. While chicken is cooking, mix flour and butter; set aside. Combine mixed vegetables, mushrooms and herbs in 2-quart casserole.

3. Whisk flour mixture into chicken mixture in skillet until smooth. Cook and stir until thickened. Add to vegetable mixture; mix well. Cover and refrigerate up to 24 hours.

4. To complete recipe, preheat oven to 450°F. Blend biscuit mix and milk in medium bowl until smooth. Drop 4 scoops batter onto chicken mixture. Bake 20 to 25 minutes or until biscuits are browned and casserole is bubbly.

Makes 4 servings

Note: This recipe can be prepared and served the same day; omit chilling. Begin checking pot pie after 18 minutes baking.

Chicken Cordon Bleu Bake

8 slices day-old white or whole-wheat bread,
    crusts removed
8 thin slices (1 ounce each) ALPINE
    LACE® Reduced Fat Swiss Cheese
2 tablespoons unsalted butter substitute
¼ cup all-purpose flour
1⅔ cups 2% low fat milk
½ teaspoon freshly ground black pepper
¼ teaspoon salt
12 thin slices (½ ounce each) skinless roasted
    chicken or turkey
12 thin slices (½ ounce each) ALPINE
    LACE® 97% Fat Free Boneless Cooked
    Ham
1 cup thin strips yellow onion

1. Preheat the oven to 350°F. Butter a 13×9×3-inch ovenproof dish. Cut each bread slice into 4 triangles, making 32. Line the bottom of the dish with 16 triangles, overlapping as you go along. Cut the cheese into 4×¼-inch strips.

2. In a medium-size saucepan, melt the butter over medium heat. Stir in the flour and cook until bubbly. Whisk in the milk, pepper and salt. Cook, whisking constantly, for 5 minutes or until slightly thickened.

3. Spread one fourth of the sauce in the baking dish. Layer one third of the chicken, one third of the cheese, one third of the ham, one third of the onion and one fourth of the sauce. Repeat 2 times. Arrange the remaining 16 triangles of bread around the edge and down the center.

4. Bake for 40 minutes or until puffy and golden. Let stand for 10 minutes.   *Makes 8 servings*

Quick Chicken Pot Pie

Chicken-Asparagus Casserole

2 teaspoons vegetable oil
1 cup chopped green or red bell peppers
1 medium onion, chopped
2 cloves garlic, minced
1 can (10¾ ounces) condensed cream of
    asparagus soup
2 eggs
1 container (8 ounces) ricotta cheese
2 cups (8 ounces) shredded Cheddar cheese,
    divided
1½ cups chopped cooked chicken cut into
    ½-inch pieces
1 package (10 ounces) frozen chopped
    asparagus,* thawed and drained
8 ounces egg noodles, cooked
    Ground black pepper (optional)

*Or, substitute ½ pound fresh asparagus cut into ½-inch pieces. Cook in simmering water 5 to 8 minutes or until crisp-tender. Drain.

1. Preheat oven to 350°F. Grease 13×9-inch casserole; set aside.

2. Heat oil in small skillet over medium heat. Add bell pepper, onion and garlic; cook and stir until crisp-tender.

3. Mix soup, eggs, ricotta cheese and 1 cup Cheddar cheese in large bowl until well blended. Add onion mixture, chicken, asparagus and noodles; mix well. Season with pepper, if desired.

4. Spread mixture evenly in prepared casserole. Top with remaining 1 cup Cheddar cheese.

5. Bake 30 minutes or until center is set and cheese is bubbly. Let stand 5 minutes before serving.   *Makes 12 servings*

Little Italy Chicken and Rice

1 package (about 4 pounds) PERDUE®
    Fresh Pick of the Chicken
1 teaspoon dried Italian herb seasoning
    Salt and ground pepper to taste
2 tablespoons olive oil
1 cup uncooked white rice
1 large onion, coarsely chopped
1 green bell pepper, seeded and diced
1 can (14½ ounces) Italian-style stewed
    tomatoes
2 cups chicken broth

Season chicken with Italian seasoning, salt and pepper. Preheat oven to 375°F. In Dutch oven over medium-high heat, heat oil. Add chicken; cook 6 to 8 minutes until brown on all sides, turning occasionally. Remove and set aside.

To drippings in pan, add rice, onion and bell pepper; sauté 2 to 3 minutes. Return chicken to Dutch oven; stir in tomatoes and chicken broth. Cover and bake in oven 45 to 50 minutes until rice is tender and chicken is cooked through.
    Makes 5 to 6 servings

Chicken-Asparagus Casserole

Indian-Spiced Chicken with Wild Rice

½ teaspoon salt
½ teaspoon ground cumin
½ teaspoon black pepper
¼ teaspoon ground cinnamon
¼ teaspoon ground turmeric
4 boneless skinless chicken breast halves
  (about 1 pound)
2 tablespoons olive oil
2 carrots, sliced
1 red bell pepper, chopped
1 rib celery, chopped
2 cloves garlic, minced
1 package (6 ounces) long grain and wild
  rice mix
2 cups reduced-sodium chicken broth
1 cup raisins
¼ cup sliced almonds
  Red bell pepper slices (optional)

COMBINE salt, cumin, black pepper, cinnamon and turmeric in small bowl. Rub spice mixture on both sides of chicken. Place chicken on plate; cover and refrigerate 30 minutes.

PREHEAT oven to 350°F. Spray 9-inch square baking dish with nonstick cooking spray.

HEAT oil in large skillet over medium-high heat until hot. Add chicken; cook 2 minutes per side or until browned. Remove chicken; set aside.

PLACE carrots, chopped bell pepper, celery and garlic in same skillet. Cook and stir 2 minutes. Add rice from mix; cook 5 minutes, stirring frequently. Add broth and seasoning packet from rice mix; bring to a boil over high heat. Remove from heat; stir in raisins. Pour into prepared dish; place chicken on rice mixture. Sprinkle with almonds.

COVER tightly with foil and bake 35 minutes or until chicken is no longer pink in center, juices run clear and rice is tender. Garnish with bell pepper slices, if desired.   *Makes 4 servings*

One-Dish Chicken 'n' Rice

1 cup uncooked regular or converted rice
1 medium red bell pepper, sliced
1 medium onion, cut into wedges
1 envelope LIPTON® Recipe Secrets®
  Golden Herb with Lemon or Savory
  Herb with Garlic Soup Mix
1½ cups water
1 cup orange juice
½ teaspoon salt
4 boneless skinless chicken breast halves
  (about 1 pound)

Preheat oven to 350°F.

In 13×9-inch casserole, combine uncooked rice, bell pepper and onion. Add Golden Herb with Lemon Soup Mix blended with water, orange juice and salt. Arrange chicken on rice, spooning some liquid over chicken. Cover and bake 45 minutes or until chicken is no longer pink in center and rice is done. Garnish with orange slices and fresh chopped parsley.

Makes 4 servings

Indian-Spiced Chicken with Wild Rice

Chicken Parmesan

4 boneless skinless chicken breast halves
2 cans (14½ ounces each) DEL MONTE®
    Italian Recipe Stewed Tomatoes
2 tablespoons cornstarch
½ teaspoon dried oregano or basil leaves
¼ teaspoon hot pepper sauce (optional)
¼ cup grated Parmesan cheese
    Chopped parsley (optional)
    Hot cooked rice or pasta (optional)

Preheat oven to 425°F. Place chicken between 2 pieces of waxed paper or plastic wrap; pound with flat side of meat mallet or rolling pin to flatten slightly. Place in 11×7-inch baking dish. Cover with foil; bake 20 minutes or until chicken is no longer pink in center. Remove foil; drain. Meanwhile, in large saucepan, combine tomatoes, cornstarch, oregano and pepper sauce. Stir to dissolve cornstarch. Cook over medium-high heat, stirring constantly, until thickened. Pour sauce over chicken; top with cheese. Return to oven; bake, uncovered, 5 minutes or until cheese is melted. Garnish with chopped parsley and serve with rice or pasta, if desired.

Makes 4 servings

Prep and cook time: 30 minutes

Pollo Verde Casserole

2 boneless skinless chicken breast halves
    (about 4 ounces each)
1 teaspoon canola oil
1 medium onion, chopped
½ medium bell pepper, chopped
1 teaspoon chopped garlic
1 cup GUILTLESS GOURMET® Green
    Tomatillo Salsa, divided
½ cup low fat sour cream, divided
    Nonstick cooking spray
1 cup (3.5 ounces) crushed GUILTLESS
    GOURMET® Unsalted Baked Tortilla
    Chips (white or yellow corn), divided

Cut chicken into 1-inch cubes. Heat oil in large skillet over medium-high heat until hot. Add chicken, onion, pepper and garlic; cook and stir 5 to 10 minutes or until chicken turns white and onion is translucent. Remove from heat.

Combine ½ cup salsa and ¼ cup sour cream in small bowl until blended. Stir salsa mixture into chicken mixture.

Preheat oven to 325°F. Coat 2-quart glass casserole dish with cooking spray. Sprinkle ½ cup crushed chips into prepared casserole dish. Spread chicken mixture over crushed chips. Top with remaining crushed chips, then with remaining ½ cup salsa.

Bake 30 minutes or cover with plastic wrap and microwave on HIGH (100% power) 12 minutes or until heated through. Let stand 5 minutes before serving. To serve, divide mixture among 4 serving plates. Top each serving with a dollop of remaining ¼ cup sour cream. *Makes 4 servings*

Chicken Parmesan

Chicken Tetrazzini

8 ounces uncooked vermicelli, broken in half
1 can (10¾ ounces) condensed cream of mushroom soup, undiluted
¼ cup half-and-half
3 tablespoons dry sherry
½ teaspoon salt
⅛ to ¼ teaspoon crushed red pepper
2 cups chopped cooked chicken breasts
1 cup frozen peas
½ cup grated Parmesan cheese
1 cup fresh coarse bread crumbs
2 tablespoons margarine or butter, melted
Chopped fresh basil (optional)
Lemon slices and lettuce leaves (optional)

PREHEAT oven to 375°F. Spray 13×9-inch baking dish with nonstick cooking spray.

COOK pasta according to package directions until al dente. Drain.

Meanwhile, **COMBINE** soup, half-and-half, sherry, salt and crushed pepper in large bowl. Stir in chicken, peas and cheese. Add pasta to chicken mixture; stir until pasta is coated. Pour into prepared dish.

COMBINE bread crumbs and margarine in small bowl. Sprinkle evenly over casserole.

BAKE, uncovered, 25 to 30 minutes or until heated through and crumbs are golden brown. Sprinkle with basil, if desired. Garnish with lemon slices and lettuce, if desired.

Makes 4 servings

Hot & Spicy Arroz con Pollo

2 tablespoons vegetable oil
1 medium onion, chopped
1 can (14½ ounces) whole tomatoes
1 can (13¾ ounces) chicken broth
1¼ cups long-grain rice
1 teaspoon salt
Pinch saffron threads (optional)
1 jar (4 ounces) chopped pimientos, drained
½ cup sliced pitted ripe olives
1 package (10 ounces) frozen peas, thawed
1 package (16 ounces) PERDUE® Fresh Hot & Spicy Chicken Wings
Water

In large deep skillet or Dutch oven over medium-high heat, heat oil. Add onion; cook 3 to 5 minutes or until tender. Stir in tomatoes with their liquid, broth, rice, salt and saffron; bring to a boil. Reduce heat to low; cover and simmer 10 minutes. Stir in pimientos, olives and peas; gently stir in chicken wings. Cover and cook 10 to 15 minutes longer or until all liquid is absorbed, rice is tender and wings are cooked through; add ¼ to ½ cup water if mixture becomes too dry. Serve hot.

Makes 5 to 6 servings

Chicken Tetrazzini

Chicken and Black Bean Enchiladas

2 jars (16 ounces each) mild picante sauce
¼ cup chopped fresh cilantro
2 tablespoons chili powder
1 teaspoon ground cumin
2 cups (10 ounces) chopped cooked chicken
1 can (15 ounces) black beans, drained and rinsed
1⅓ cups (2.8-ounce can) FRENCH'S® French Fried Onions, divided
1 package (about 10 ounces) flour tortillas (7 inches)
1 cup (4 ounces) shredded Monterey Jack cheese with jalapeño peppers

Preheat oven to 350°F. Grease 10×15-inch jelly-roll baking pan. Combine picante sauce, cilantro, chili powder and cumin in large saucepan. Bring to a boil. Reduce heat to low; simmer 5 minutes.

Combine *1½ cups* sauce mixture, chicken, beans and ⅔ *cup* French Fried Onions in medium bowl. Spoon *a scant ½ cup* filling over bottom third of each tortilla. Roll-up tortillas enclosing filling and arrange, seam side down, in a single layer in bottom of prepared baking pan. Spoon remaining sauce evenly over tortillas.

Bake, uncovered, 20 minutes or until heated through. Sprinkle with remaining ⅔ *cup* onions and cheese. Bake 5 minutes or until cheese is melted and onions are golden. Serve immediately.

Makes 5 to 6 servings

Prep time: 45 minutes
Cook time: 25 minutes

Savory Chicken & Biscuits

2 tablespoons olive or vegetable oil
1 pound boneless, skinless chicken breasts, cut into 1-inch pieces
1 medium onion, chopped
1 cup thinly sliced carrots
1 cup thinly sliced celery
1 envelope LIPTON® Recipe Secrets® Savory Herb with Garlic Soup Mix
1 cup milk
1 package (10 ounces) refrigerated flaky buttermilk biscuits

Preheat oven to 375°F.

In 12-inch skillet, heat oil over medium-high heat. Add chicken; cook 5 minutes or until no longer pink. Stir in onion, carrots and celery; cook, stirring occasionally, 3 minutes. Stir in Savory Herb with Garlic Soup Mix blended with milk. Bring to a boil over medium-high heat, stirring occasionally; cook 1 minute. Turn into lightly greased 2-quart casserole; arrange biscuits on top of chicken mixture with edges touching. Bake 15 minutes or until biscuits are golden brown.

Makes 4 servings

Note: This recipe is also terrific with LIPTON® Recipe Secrets® Golden Onion or Golden Herb with Lemon Soup Mix.

Chicken and Black Bean Enchiladas

Chicken & Rice Bake

1 can (10¾ ounces) condensed cream of
    mushroom soup
1¾ cups water
¾ cup uncooked long-grain rice
1½ cups sliced mushrooms
1⅓ cups (2.8-ounce can) FRENCH'S® French
    Fried Onions, divided
4 teaspoons FRENCH'S® Worcestershire
    Sauce, divided
4 chicken breast halves (about 2 pounds)
½ teaspoon *each* paprika and dried thyme
    leaves

Preheat oven to 375°F. Combine soup, water,
rice, mushrooms, ⅔ *cup* French Fried Onions and
2 teaspoons Worcestershire in 3-quart oblong
baking dish. Arrange chicken over rice mixture.
Brush chicken with remaining Worcestershire
and sprinkle with paprika and thyme.

Bake, uncovered, 1 hour or until chicken is no
longer pink in center. Top with remaining ⅔ *cup*
onions. Bake 3 minutes or until onions are
golden.   *Makes 4 servings*

Prep time: 10 minutes

Cook time: about 1 hour

Tip: Remove skin from chicken before baking, if
desired.

Chicken Pot Pie

2 tablespoons butter or margarine
1 pound boneless, skinless chicken thighs,
    cut into 1-inch pieces (about 2 cups)*
2 ribs celery, sliced
2 carrots, cut lengthwise in half and sliced
1 medium onion, diced
1 cup frozen cut green beans, thawed
1 envelope LIPTON® Recipe Secrets®
    Savory Herb with Garlic or Golden
    Onion Soup Mix
1 cup milk
1 refrigerated pie crust or pastry for
    single-crust pie

*Use 2 cups cut-up cooked chicken or turkey and
eliminate melting butter and cooking chicken.

Preheat oven to 400°F.

In 10-inch skillet, melt butter over medium-high
heat and cook chicken, stirring frequently, 8
minutes or until no longer pink. With slotted
spoon, remove chicken to 9-inch pie plate.

In same skillet, stir celery, carrots and onion;
cook 8 minutes. Stir in green beans and Savory
Herb with Garlic Soup Mix blended with milk;
bring to a boil over medium-high heat. Turn into
pie plate with chicken; top with crust and seal
edges tightly. Pierce crust with fork. Bake 25
minutes or until golden. Let stand 10 minutes
before serving.   *Makes about 4 servings*

Menu Suggestion: Serve with your favorite
LIPTON® Soup and LIPTON® Iced Tea.

Chicken & Rice Bake

Chicken Fiesta

2½ to 3 pounds chicken pieces
  Salt
  Pepper
  Paprika
 2 tablespoons butter or margarine
 ¼ pound pork sausage
 ¾ cup sliced celery
 ¾ cup sliced green onions with tops
 3 cups cooked rice
 1 can (12 ounces) whole kernel corn with
    peppers, drained
 2 teaspoons lemon juice

Season chicken with salt, pepper and paprika. In large skillet, melt butter. Add chicken to skillet; brown well. Drain chicken on paper towels; set aside. Cook sausage, celery and onions in same skillet over medium-high heat, stirring frequently until vegetables are crisp-tender. Add rice, corn and lemon juice; mix well. Pour into shallow baking dish. Arrange chicken on top of rice mixture, pressing chicken slightly into rice mixture. Cover with foil. Bake 30 to 40 minutes or until chicken is no longer pink in center.

Makes 6 servings

Favorite recipe from **USA Rice Federation**

Oven Chicken & Rice

 1 can (10¾ ounces) condensed cream of
    mushroom soup
 1 cup long-grain or converted rice
 1 teaspoon dried dill weed, divided
 ¼ teaspoon black pepper
 1 (3-pound) chicken, cut up and skinned
 ½ cup crushed multi-grain crackers
 1 teaspoon paprika
 2 tablespoons butter or margarine, melted
  Fresh dill sprigs for garnish

PREHEAT oven to 375°F. Combine soup, 1⅓ cups water, rice, ¾ teaspoon dill weed and pepper in 13×9-inch baking dish. Arrange chicken pieces on top of rice mixture. Cover tightly with foil. Bake 45 minutes.

SPRINKLE chicken pieces with crackers, paprika and remaining ¼ teaspoon dill. Drizzle with butter. Bake 5 to 10 minutes or until chicken is tender. Season to taste with salt and pepper. Garnish with dill sprig, if desired.

Makes 4 to 5 servings

Terrific
ONE-DISH MEALS

Coq au Vin

½ cup all-purpose flour
1¼ teaspoons salt
¾ teaspoon black pepper
3½ pounds chicken pieces
2 tablespoons margarine or butter
8 ounces mushrooms, cut in half if large
4 cloves garlic, minced
¾ cup chicken broth
¾ cup dry red wine
2 teaspoons dried thyme leaves
1½ pounds red potatoes, quartered
2 cups frozen pearl onions (about 8 ounces)
Chopped fresh parsley (optional)

PREHEAT oven to 350°F.

COMBINE flour, salt and pepper in large resealable plastic food storage bag. Add chicken, two pieces at a time, and seal bag. Shake to coat chicken; remove chicken and set aside. Repeat with remaining pieces. Reserve remaining flour mixture.

MELT margarine in ovenproof Dutch oven over medium-high heat. Arrange chicken in single layer in Dutch oven and cook 3 minutes per side or until browned. Transfer to plate; set aside. Repeat with remaining pieces.

ADD mushrooms and garlic to Dutch oven; cook and stir 2 minutes. Sprinkle reserved flour mixture over mushroom mixture; cook and stir 1 minute. Add broth, wine and thyme; bring to a boil over high heat, stirring to scrape browned bits from bottom of Dutch oven. Add potatoes and onions; return to a boil. Remove from heat and place chicken in Dutch oven, partially covering chicken with broth mixture.

BAKE, covered, about 45 minutes or until chicken is no longer pink in center, juices run clear and sauce is slightly thickened. Transfer chicken and vegetables to shallow bowls. Spoon sauce over chicken and vegetables. Sprinkle with parsley, if desired.   *Makes 4 to 6 servings*

Serving Suggestion: Serve with assorted fresh baked rolls.

Coq au Vin

Rotelle with Grilled Chicken Dijon

¾ cup GREY POUPON® Dijon Mustard,
    divided
1 tablespoon lemon juice
1 tablespoon olive oil
1 clove garlic, minced
½ teaspoon Italian seasoning
1 pound boneless, skinless chicken breasts
¼ cup margarine or butter
1 cup chicken broth or lower sodium
    chicken broth
1 cup chopped cooked broccoli
⅓ cup coarsely chopped roasted red peppers
1 pound tri-color rotelle or spiral-shaped
    pasta, cooked
¼ cup grated Parmesan cheese

In medium bowl, combine ¼ cup mustard, lemon juice, oil, garlic and Italian seasoning. Add chicken, stirring to coat well. Refrigerate for 1 hour.

Grill or broil chicken over medium heat for 6 minutes on each side or until done. Cool slightly; slice into ½-inch strips and set aside.

In large skillet, over medium heat, melt margarine or butter; blend in remaining mustard and chicken broth. Stir in broccoli and peppers; heat through. In large serving bowl, combine hot cooked pasta, broccoli mixture, chicken and Parmesan cheese, tossing to coat well. Garnish as desired. Serve immediately.   *Makes 5 servings*

One-Pot Chicken Couscous

¼ cup olive oil
2 pounds boneless, skinless chicken breasts,
    cut into 1-inch chunks
4 large carrots, peeled and sliced
2 medium onions, diced
2 large cloves garlic, minced
2 cans (13¾ ounces each) chicken broth
2 cups couscous
2 teaspoons TABASCO® pepper sauce
½ teaspoon salt
1 cup raisins or currants
1 cup slivered almonds, toasted
¼ cup fresh chopped parsley or mint

In 12-inch skillet over medium-high heat, in hot oil, cook chicken until well browned on all sides. With slotted spoon, remove chicken to plate. Reduce heat to medium. In drippings remaining in skillet, cook carrots and onion 5 minutes. Add garlic; cook 2 minutes longer, stirring frequently.

Add chicken broth, couscous, TABASCO® sauce, salt and chicken chunks. Heat to boiling, then reduce heat to low, cover and simmer 5 minutes. Stir in raisins, almonds and parsley.
                                    Makes 8 servings

Rotelle with Grilled Chicken Dijon

Chicken Marsala

6 ounces uncooked broad egg noodles
½ cup Italian-style dry bread crumbs
1 teaspoon dried basil leaves
1 egg
1 teaspoon water
4 boneless skinless chicken breast halves
3 tablespoons olive oil, divided
¾ cup chopped onion
8 ounces cremini or button mushrooms,
    sliced
3 cloves garlic, minced
3 tablespoons all-purpose flour
1 can (14½ ounces) chicken broth
½ cup dry marsala wine
¾ teaspoon salt
¼ teaspoon black pepper
    Chopped fresh parsley (optional)

PREHEAT oven to 375°F. Spray 11×7-inch baking dish with nonstick cooking spray. Cook noodles according to package directions until al dente. Drain and place in prepared dish.

Meanwhile, **COMBINE** bread crumbs and basil on shallow plate or pie plate. Beat egg with water on another shallow plate or pie plate. Dip chicken in egg mixture, letting excess drip off. Roll in crumb mixture, patting to coat. Heat 2 tablespoons oil in large skillet over medium-high heat until hot. Cook chicken 3 minutes per side or until browned. Transfer to clean plate; set aside.

HEAT remaining 1 tablespoon oil in same skillet over medium heat. Add onion; cook and stir 5 minutes. Add mushrooms and garlic; cook and stir 3 minutes. Sprinkle flour over onion mixture;

cook and stir 1 minute. Add broth, wine, salt and pepper; bring to a boil over high heat. Cook and stir 5 minutes or until sauce thickens. Reserve ½ cup sauce. Pour remaining sauce over noodles; stir until noodles are well coated. Place chicken on top of noodles. Spoon reserved sauce over chicken.

BAKE, uncovered, 20 minutes or until chicken is no longer pink in center. Sprinkle with parsley, if desired. *Makes 4 servings*

Southwest Skillet

1 cup cubed, cooked chicken breast
1 bag (16 ounces) BIRDS EYE® frozen
    Pasta Secrets™ Zesty Garlic
1 cup chunky salsa
½ cup chopped green or red bell pepper
½ teaspoon chili powder

• In large skillet, combine all ingredients.

• Cook over medium heat 10 to 15 minutes or until heated through. *Makes 4 servings*

Prep time: 5 minutes

Cook time: 15 minutes

Cheesy Southwest Skillet: Stir in ½ cup shredded Cheddar cheese during last 5 minutes. Cook until cheese is melted.

Creamy Southwest Skillet: Remove skillet from heat. Stir in ¼ cup sour cream before serving.

Chicken Marsala

Chicken Curry

½ cup uncooked rice
1 small onion
2 boneless skinless chicken breast halves
1 tablespoon butter or margarine
1 clove garlic, minced
1 teaspoon curry powder
¼ teaspoon ground ginger
3 tablespoons raisins
1 cup coarsely chopped apple, divided
1 teaspoon chicken bouillon granules
¼ cup plain nonfat yogurt
2 teaspoons all-purpose flour

1. Cook rice according to package directions.

2. While rice is cooking, cut onion into thin slices. Cut chicken into ¾-inch cubes.

3. Heat butter, garlic, curry powder and ginger in medium skillet over medium heat. Add chicken; cook and stir 2 minutes. Add onion, raisins and ¾ cup chopped apple; cook and stir 3 minutes. Stir in chicken bouillon and ¼ cup water. Reduce heat to low; cover and cook 2 minutes.

4. Combine yogurt and flour in small bowl. Stir several tablespoons liquid from skillet into yogurt mixture. Cook and stir just until mixture starts to boil.

5. Serve chicken curry over rice; garnish with remaining ¼ cup chopped apple.

Makes 2 servings

Prep and cook time: 28 minutes

For a special touch, sprinkle chicken with green onion slivers just before serving.

Mexican Chicken Stew

1 tablespoon olive oil
1 pound boneless, skinless chicken breasts, cut into ½-inch cubes
1 can (16 ounces) whole-kernel corn, drained
1 can (15 ounces) red kidney beans, undrained
1 can (15 ounces) black beans, drained and rinsed
1 can (4 ounces) chopped green chilies, undrained
1 cup chicken broth
1½ teaspoons MCCORMICK®/SCHILLING® California Style Garlic Powder
1½ teaspoons MCCORMICK®/SCHILLING® Ground Cumin
1 teaspoon MCCORMICK®/SCHILLING® Oregano Leaves
1 teaspoon MCCORMICK®/SCHILLING® Chili Powder
½ cup sliced scallions
  Red bell pepper cut into flower shapes for garnish, (optional)

1. Heat oil in large skillet over medium-high heat. Add chicken; cook 5 minutes. Remove chicken from skillet; set aside.

2. Add remaining ingredients except scallions and garnish to skillet and stir to mix well. Heat to a boil. Reduce heat to medium; cover and cook 10 minutes.

3. Stir in chicken and scallions. Cover and simmer 5 to 10 minutes. Garnish, if desired.

Makes 6 servings

Chicken Curry

Lemon Chicken with Walnuts

¼ cup FILIPPO BERIO® Olive Oil, divided
½ cup chopped walnuts
4 boneless skinless chicken breast halves, pounded thin
2 tablespoons all-purpose flour
1 medium onion, chopped
1 clove garlic, minced
1 cup dry white wine
2 carrots, very thinly sliced
¼ cup lemon juice
½ teaspoon dried thyme leaves
1 zucchini, very thinly sliced
1 yellow squash, very thinly sliced
Chopped fresh parsley

In large skillet, heat 2 tablespoons olive oil over medium-high heat until hot. Add walnuts; cook and stir 2 to 3 minutes or until lightly browned. Remove with slotted spoon; reserve. Lightly coat chicken breasts in flour. Add remaining 2 tablespoons olive oil to skillet; heat over medium-high heat until hot. Add chicken, onion and garlic; cook 5 minutes or until chicken is brown, turning chicken and stirring occasionally. Add wine, carrots, lemon juice and thyme. Cover; reduce heat to low and simmer 8 minutes. Add zucchini and squash; cover and simmer 2 minutes or until vegetables are tender-crisp and chicken is no longer pink in center. Remove chicken and vegetables; keep warm. Boil sauce until slightly thickened. Pour over chicken and vegetables. Top with reserved walnuts and parsley.

Makes 4 servings

Drunken Chicken

½ cup all-purpose flour
½ teaspoon salt
½ teaspoon ground black pepper
1 (3-pound) chicken, cut into 8 pieces, skin removed
3 tablespoons vegetable oil, divided
1 medium onion, sliced
2 cups quartered mushrooms
1 teaspoon minced garlic
1 (13¾-fluid ounce) can COLLEGE INN® chicken broth
½ cup REGINA® Burgundy Cooking Wine
Hot cooked egg noodles
2 tablespoons chopped fresh parsley

Combine flour, salt and pepper. Coat chicken with seasoned flour, shaking off excess. In large skillet, over medium-high heat, brown chicken in 2 tablespoons oil; remove chicken from skillet.

In same skillet, over medium heat, sauté onion in remaining oil for 2 minutes. Add mushrooms and garlic; sauté for 2 minutes. Add chicken broth, wine and browned chicken parts to skillet. Heat to a boil; reduce heat. Cover; simmer for 35 to 40 minutes or until chicken is no longer pink. Serve over noodles garnished with parsley.

Makes 6 servings

Lemon Chicken with Walnuts

Chicken Tetrazzini with Roasted Red Peppers

6 ounces uncooked egg noodles
3 tablespoons margarine or butter
¼ cup all-purpose flour
1 can (about 14 ounces) chicken broth
1 cup whipping cream
2 tablespoons dry sherry
2 cans (6 ounces each) sliced mushrooms, drained
1 jar (7½ ounces) roasted red peppers, cut into ½-inch strips
2 cups chopped cooked chicken
1 teaspoon Italian seasoning
½ cup grated Parmesan cheese

1. Cook noodles according to package directions; drain.

2. While noodles are cooking, melt margarine in medium saucepan over medium heat. Add flour and whisk until smooth. Add chicken broth; bring to a boil over high heat. Remove from heat. Gradually add whipping cream and sherry; stir to combine.

3. Combine mushrooms, red peppers and noodles in large bowl; toss to combine. Add half the chicken broth mixture to noodle mixture. Combine remaining chicken broth mixture, chicken and Italian seasoning in large bowl.

4. Spoon noodle mixture into serving dish. Make a well in center of noodles and spoon in chicken mixture. Sprinkle with cheese.

Makes 6 servings

Prep and cook time: 20 minutes

Chicken & Pasta Toss with Sun-Dried Tomatoes

4 boneless skinless chicken breast halves (about 1¼ pounds), cut into strips
1 cup prepared GOOD SEASONS® Roasted Garlic or Italian Salad Dressing, divided
1 pound bow tie pasta
3 cups broccoli flowerets
1 cup sun-dried tomatoes in olive oil
½ cup (2 ounces) KRAFT® 100% Grated Parmesan Cheese

COOK chicken in ¼ cup of the dressing on medium heat until cooked through, about 8 minutes.

COOK pasta as directed on package, adding broccoli to water during last 3 minutes of cooking time. Drain pasta and broccoli.

TOSS pasta, broccoli and chicken with remaining ingredients. Season to taste with salt and pepper.

Makes 4 to 6 servings

Prep time: 15 minutes
Cook time: 12 minutes

Chicken Tetrazzini with Roasted Red Peppers

Creole Chicken

3 tablespoons vegetable oil, divided
1 whole chicken, cut up *or* 2 pounds
   chicken pieces
1 medium onion, thinly sliced
2 teaspoons LAWRY'S® Garlic Powder with
   Parsley
1½ teaspoons LAWRY'S® Seasoned Salt
1 teaspoon LAWRY'S® Seasoned Pepper
1 can (8 ounces) tomato sauce
½ cup red wine
3 medium tomatoes, chopped
2 bell peppers (red or green), sliced into
   strips

In large skillet, heat oil. Add chicken and brown over medium-high heat; remove and set aside. In same skillet, add onion and sauté over medium-high heat until tender. Add Garlic Powder with Parsley, Seasoned Salt and Seasoned Pepper. Return chicken pieces to skillet. Add remaining ingredients. Cover and simmer over low heat 30 to 40 minutes until chicken is cooked.

Makes 4 to 6 servings

Meal Suggestion: Serve over hot cooked white rice with crusty French bread and iced tea.

Chili Pepper Pasta Santa Fe Style

1 package (12 ounces) PASTA LABELLA®
   Chili Pepper Pasta
¼ cup extra-virgin olive oil
12 ounces boneless skinless chicken breasts,
   julienned
1½ teaspoons cracked black pepper
1 cup julienned yellow bell pepper
1 cup sliced leeks
1 cup julienned jicama
1 teaspoon minced garlic
⅓ cup chopped fresh cilantro
1 teaspoon dried oregano leaves
¾ cup chicken broth
⅓ cup grated Romano cheese
   Salt to taste

Cook pasta according to package directions. Heat olive oil in large skillet over medium heat. Add chicken and black pepper. Cook and stir for 4 minutes. Add bell pepper, leeks, jicama, garlic, cilantro and oregano; cook for 5 minutes. Add chicken broth; simmer for 3 minutes. Mix with hot pasta. Sprinkle with cheese and serve.

Makes 3 servings

Creole Chicken

Southern-Style Chicken and Greens

1 teaspoon salt
1 teaspoon paprika
½ teaspoon black pepper
3½ pounds chicken pieces
4 thick slices smoked bacon (4 ounces),
    cut crosswise into ¼-inch pieces
1 cup uncooked rice
1 can (14½ ounces) stewed tomatoes,
    undrained
1¼ cups chicken broth
2 cups packed coarsely chopped fresh
    collard or mustard greens or kale
    (3 to 4 ounces)
Tomato wedges and fresh Italian parsley
    (optional)

PREHEAT oven to 350°F.

COMBINE salt, paprika and pepper in small bowl. Sprinkle meaty side of chicken pieces with salt mixture; set aside.

PLACE bacon in ovenproof Dutch oven; cook over medium heat until crisp. Drain on paper towels. Reserve bacon fat. Heat bacon fat over medium-high heat until hot. Arrange chicken in single layer in Dutch oven and cook 3 minutes per side or until browned. Transfer to clean plate; set aside. Repeat with remaining pieces. Reserve 1 tablespoon bacon fat in Dutch oven; discard remaining bacon fat.

ADD rice to Dutch oven; cook and stir 1 minute. Add tomatoes with juice, broth, collard greens and half of bacon; bring to a boil over high heat. Remove from heat; arrange chicken over rice mixture.

BAKE, covered, about 40 minutes or until chicken is no longer pink in centers, juices run clear and most of liquid is absorbed. Let stand 5 minutes before serving. Transfer to serving platter; sprinkle with remaining bacon. Garnish with tomato and Italian parsley, if desired.

Makes 4 to 6 servings

Jiffy Chicken Supper

1 bag (16 ounces) BIRDS EYE® frozen
    Pasta Secrets™ White Cheddar or
    Creamy Peppercorn
¼ cup water
1 can (6½ ounces) chicken, drained
¼ cup pitted ripe olives, sliced
1 cup (8 ounces) plain yogurt
2 tablespoons chopped fresh parsley

• In large skillet, place Pasta Secrets and water. Bring to boil over high heat. Reduce heat to medium; cover and simmer 7 to 9 minutes or until pasta is tender.

• Stir in chicken and olives; cook 5 minutes more.

• In small bowl, combine yogurt and parsley.

• Stir yogurt mixture into Pasta Secrets mixture; cover and cook over low heat 1 minute or until heated through.   *Makes 4 servings*

Prep time: 5 minutes

Cook time: 15 to 18 minutes

Southern-Style Chicken and Greens

Ortega® Chicken Fajitas

2 tablespoons vegetable oil
1½ cups (1 medium) sliced onion
1 cup (1 medium) red bell pepper strips
1 cup (1 medium) green bell pepper strips
1 pound (about 4) boneless, skinless chicken breasts, cut into ¼-inch strips
2½ cups (24-ounce jar) ORTEGA® Thick & Chunky Salsa, hot, medium or mild, or Garden Style Salsa, medium or mild, divided
2 tablespoons ORTEGA® Diced Jalapeños (optional)
½ cup (6-ounce container) frozen guacamole, thawed
8 soft taco-size (8-inch) flour tortillas, warmed
1 cup (4 ounces) shredded Monterey Jack cheese

HEAT oil in medium skillet over medium-high heat. Add onion and bell peppers; cook, stirring constantly, for 3 to 4 minutes or until tender. Remove from skillet. Add chicken to skillet; cook, stirring constantly, for 4 to 5 minutes or until no longer pink in center. Add cooked vegetables, *1 cup* salsa and jalapeños; heat through.

SPREAD 1 tablespoon guacamole onto each tortilla. Top with ½ cup chicken mixture and 2 tablespoons cheese; fold into burritos. Serve with *remaining 1½ cups* salsa.   *Makes 8 fajitas*

Lemon Pepper Pasta with Chicken and Dijon Teriyaki Sauce

1 package (12 ounces) PASTA LABELLA® Lemon Pepper Penne Rigate
¼ cup olive oil
9 ounces boneless skinless chicken breasts, cut into 1-inch cubes
½ cup sliced red onion
1½ cups broccoli florets
1 cup sliced mushrooms
1 tablespoon chopped garlic
1½ teaspoon ground ginger
¼ teaspoon salt
¼ teaspoon black pepper
1½ cups chicken broth
5 tablespoons Dijon mustard
¼ cup teriyaki sauce
¼ cup minced green onions

Cook pasta according to package directions. Meanwhile, heat olive oil in large skillet or saucepan over medium heat; sauté chicken for 5 minutes. Add onion, broccoli, mushrooms, garlic, ginger, salt and pepper. Continue to cook for 8 minutes. Add chicken broth; bring mixture to a simmer. Whisk in mustard and teriyaki sauce. Cook until sauce is of medium-thin consistency. Add hot pasta; mix well and heat thoroughly. Serve sprinkled with green onions.

Makes 4 servings

Ortega® Chicken Fajitas

Arroz con Pollo

4 slices bacon
1½ pounds (about 6) boneless, skinless
    chicken breasts
1 cup (1 small) chopped onion
1 cup (1 small) chopped green bell pepper
2 large cloves garlic, finely chopped
2 cups long-grain white rice
2½ cups (24-ounce jar) ORTEGA® Garden
    Style Salsa, mild
1¾ cups (14½-ounce can) chicken broth
1 cup (8-ounce can) CONTADINA®
    Tomato Sauce
1 teaspoon salt
½ teaspoon ground cumin
    Chopped fresh parsley

COOK bacon in large saucepan over medium-
high heat until crispy; remove from saucepan.
Crumble bacon; set aside. Add chicken to
saucepan; cook, turning frequently, for 5 to 7
minutes or until golden on both sides. Remove
from saucepan; keep warm. Discard all but 2
tablespoons drippings from saucepan.

ADD onion, bell pepper and garlic; cook for
3 to 4 minutes or until crisp-tender. Add rice;
cook for 2 to 3 minutes. Stir in salsa, chicken
broth, tomato sauce, salt and cumin. Bring to a
boil. Place chicken over rice mixture; reduce heat
to low. Cover. Cook for 20 to 25 minutes or until
most of moisture is absorbed and chicken is no
longer pink in center. Sprinkle with bacon and
parsley. *Makes 4 to 6 servings*

Chicken Pasta

2 skinless, boneless chicken breasts
    (12 ounces)
1 tablespoon CHEF PAUL
    PRUDHOMME'S Meat Magic®, divided
6 ounces fettuccine or angel hair pasta*
1 cup chopped white onions
½ cup chopped celery
½ cup chopped green bell pepper
2 cups defatted chicken stock, divided
2 tablespoons flour
3 cups thinly sliced fresh mushrooms
1 teaspoon minced garlic
½ cup chopped green onions

*Substitute your favorite pasta for fettuccine or angel hair.

Cut chicken into thin strips; place in small bowl.
Add 2 teaspoons Meat Magic; toss to combine.
Cook pasta according to package directions.

Place large skillet over high heat; add white
onions, celery, bell pepper and remaining 1
teaspoon Meat Magic. Cook over high heat,
shaking skillet and stirring occasionally for 5
minutes. *Don't scrape skillet!* Add ½ cup chicken
stock; cook 4 minutes, scraping up browned
coating on bottom of the skillet. Stir in chicken
mixture; cook 4 minutes. Add flour and stir well;
cook 2 minutes. Gently stir in mushrooms and
garlic so mushrooms don't break. Add ½ cup
chicken stock; cook 4 minutes, scraping any
browned coating from skillet bottom. Add ½ cup
stock; cook 5 minutes, stirring and scraping
skillet. Add green onions and remaining ½ cup
stock. Stir and scrape skillet well. Cook 5 more
minutes; remove from heat. *Makes 6 servings*

Arroz con Pollo

Mexicali Chicken Stew

1 package (1.25 ounces) taco seasoning, divided
12 ounces boneless skinless chicken thighs
2 cans (14½ ounces each) stewed tomatoes with onions, celery and green peppers
1 package (9 ounces) frozen green beans
1 package (10 ounces) frozen corn
4 cups tortilla chips

1. Place half of taco seasoning in small bowl. Cut chicken thighs into 1-inch pieces; coat with taco seasoning.

2. Coat large nonstick skillet with nonstick cooking spray. Cook and stir chicken 5 minutes over medium heat. Add tomatoes, beans, corn and remaining taco seasoning; bring to a boil. Reduce heat to medium-low; simmer 10 minutes. Top with tortilla chips before serving.

Makes 4 servings

Prep and cook time: 20 minutes

Serving Suggestion: Whip up nachos in a flash to serve along with the stew. Spread some of the tortilla chips on a plate; dot with salsa and sprinkle with cheese. Heat just until cheese is melted.

Snappy Chicken and Vegetables

1 tablespoon vegetable oil
3 teaspoons MCCORMICK®/SCHILLING® Chicken & Fish Seasoning, divided
1 pound boneless, skinless chicken breasts (4 half breasts)
4 cups assorted sliced fresh vegetables, such as onion, zucchini, yellow squash, broccoli and tomato
Juice of ½ lemon (optional)

1. Heat oil in nonstick skillet over medium-high heat. Stir in 2 teaspoons seasoning.

2. Add chicken to skillet and cook 4 to 5 minutes. Turn chicken over. Cover; reduce heat to medium. Cook 5 minutes or until chicken is no longer pink in center. Remove chicken; cover and keep warm.

3. Add vegetables to skillet; sprinkle with remaining 1 teaspoon seasoning. Sauté about 4 minutes or until vegetables are crisp-tender.

4. Place chicken breasts on warm serving platter; surround with vegetables. Sprinkle chicken with lemon juice, if desired.

Makes 4 servings (1½ cups each)

Mexicali Chicken Stew

Chicken in Cream Sauce

4 boneless skinless chicken breast halves
   (about 1¼ pounds), cut into strips
1 medium red pepper, cut into strips
¼ cup sliced green onions
1 teaspoon Italian seasoning
½ teaspoon salt
2 tablespoons butter or margarine
¼ cup dry white wine, divided
1 package (8 ounces) PHILADELPHIA
   BRAND® Cream Cheese, cubed
½ cup milk
8 ounces linguine, cooked, drained

COOK chicken, vegetables and seasonings
in butter in medium skillet on medium heat
10 minutes or until chicken is cooked through,
stirring occasionally. Add 2 tablespoons of the
wine; simmer 5 minutes.

STIR cream cheese, milk and remaining
2 tablespoons wine in small saucepan on low
heat until smooth.

PLACE hot linguine on serving platter; top with
chicken mixture and cream cheese mixture.
Garnish, if desired.   *Makes 4 to 6 servings*

Prep time: 20 minutes
Cook time: 20 minutes

Country Chicken Stew

6 slices bacon, diced
2 leeks, chopped (white party only) (about
   ½ pound)
3 shallots, chopped
1 medium carrot, cut into ¼-inch pieces
1½ pounds boneless skinless chicken thighs,
   cut into 1-inch pieces
1½ pounds boneless skinless chicken breasts,
   cut into 1-inch pieces
½ pound boneless smoked pork butt, cut into
   1-inch pieces
1 Granny Smith apple, cored and diced
2 cups dry white wine or chicken broth
1½ teaspoons herbes de Provence, crushed*
1 teaspoon salt
   Black pepper to taste
2 bay leaves
2 cans (15 ounces) cannellini beans or great
   Northern beans, drained

*If herbes de Provence is not available, substitute ¼
teaspoon *each* rubbed sage, dried rosemary, thyme,
oregano, marjoram and basil leaves.

Cook and stir bacon in 5-quart Dutch oven over
medium-high heat until crisp. Add leeks, shallots
and carrot; cook and stir vegetables until leeks
and shallots are soft. Stir in chicken, pork, apple,
wine and seasonings. Bring to a boil over high
heat. Reduce heat to low. Cover and simmer
30 minutes.

Stir in beans. Cover and simmer 25 minutes more
until chicken and pork are fork-tender and
chicken is no longer pink in center. Remove bay
leaves before serving.   *Makes 8 to 10 servings*

Chicken in Cream Sauce

Creole Chicken Thighs & Rice

2 tablespoons vegetable oil
2¼ pounds chicken thighs
½ teaspoon salt
½ teaspoon paprika
½ teaspoon dried thyme leaves
¼ teaspoon black pepper
½ cup chopped onion
½ cup chopped green bell pepper
½ cup chopped celery
2 cloves garlic, minced
1 cup long-grain or converted rice
1 can (14½ ounces) diced tomatoes,
    undrained
Hot pepper sauce
Fresh thyme sprigs for garnish

HEAT oil in large skillet or Dutch oven over medium heat until hot. Add chicken; sprinkle with salt, paprika, thyme and black pepper. Cook 5 to 6 minutes on each side or until golden brown. Remove from skillet.

ADD onion, bell pepper, celery and garlic to same skillet; cook and stir 2 minutes. Add rice; cook 2 minutes. Stir in tomatoes with juice, 1 cup water and hot pepper sauce; bring to a boil.

ARRANGE chicken over rice mixture. Reduce heat. Cover and simmer 20 minutes or until chicken is no longer pink in center, juices run clear and liquid is absorbed. Garnish with thyme sprigs, if desired. *Makes 4 servings*

Chicken Provençale

1 tablespoon olive oil
2 pounds skinless chicken thighs
½ cup sliced onion
½ cup sliced green bell pepper
2 cloves garlic, minced
1 pound eggplant, peeled and cut into
    ¼-inch-thick slices
2 medium tomatoes, cut into ¼-inch-thick
    slices
¼ cup chopped fresh parsley *or*
    2 teaspoons dried parsley
¼ cup chopped fresh basil *or* 2 teaspoons
    dried basil leaves
1 teaspoon salt
1 cup reduced-sodium chicken broth
½ cup dry white wine
Fresh parsley sprigs for garnish

HEAT oil in large skillet over medium-high heat until hot. Add chicken; cook 2 to 3 minutes on each side or until browned. Remove chicken from skillet.

ADD onion, bell pepper and garlic to same skillet; cook and stir 3 to 4 minutes or until onion is tender.

RETURN chicken to skillet. Arrange eggplant and tomato slices over chicken. Sprinkle with parsley, basil and salt. Add chicken broth and wine; bring to a boil. Reduce heat; cover and simmer 45 to 50 minutes or until chicken is no longer pink in center and juices run clear. Garnish with parsley sprigs, if desired.
Makes 6 servings

Creole Chicken Thighs & Rice

Tasty

ROASTING, GRILLING & MORE

Stuffed Chicken with Apple Glaze

 1 broiler-fryer chicken (3½ to 4 pounds)
 ½ teaspoon salt
 ¼ teaspoon pepper
 2 tablespoons vegetable oil
 1 package (6 ounces) chicken-flavored stuffing mix, plus ingredients to prepare mix
 1 cup chopped apple
 ¼ cup chopped walnuts
 ¼ cup raisins
 ¼ cup thinly sliced celery
 ½ teaspoon grated lemon peel
 ½ cup apple jelly
 1 tablespoon lemon juice
 ½ teaspoon ground cinnamon

Preheat oven to 350°F. Sprinkle inside of chicken with salt and pepper; rub outside with oil.

Prepare stuffing mix in large bowl according to package directions. Add apple, walnuts, raisins, celery and lemon peel; mix well. Stuff body cavity loosely with stuffing.* Place chicken in baking pan. Cover loosely with foil; roast 1 hour.

Meanwhile, combine jelly, lemon juice and cinnamon in small saucepan. Simmer over low heat 3 minutes or until blended. Remove foil from chicken; brush with jelly glaze. Roast chicken, uncovered, brushing frequently with jelly glaze, 30 minutes or until meat thermometer inserted into thickest part of thigh registers 185°F and juices run clear. Let chicken stand 15 minutes before carving.   *Makes 4 servings*

*Bake any leftover stuffing in covered casserole alongside chicken until heated through.

Favorite recipe from **Delmarva Poultry Industry, Inc.**

Stuffed Chicken with Apple Glaze

Broiled Chicken with Honeyed Onion Sauce

2 pounds boneless skinless chicken thighs
4 teaspoons olive oil, divided
1 teaspoon salt, divided
1 teaspoon paprika
1 teaspoon dried oregano leaves
½ teaspoon ground cumin
¼ teaspoon black pepper
1 onion, sliced
2 cloves garlic, minced
¼ cup golden raisins
¼ cup honey
2 tablespoons lemon juice

1. Preheat broiler. Rub chicken with 2 teaspoons olive oil. Combine ½ teaspoon salt, paprika, oregano, cumin and pepper; rub mixture over chicken.

2. Place chicken on broiler pan. Broil about 6 inches from heat source 5 minutes per side or until chicken is no longer pink in center.

3. While chicken is cooking, heat remaining 2 teaspoons oil in medium nonstick skillet. Add onion and garlic; cook about 8 minutes or until onion is dark golden brown, stirring occasionally.

4. Stir in raisins, honey, lemon juice, ¼ cup water and remaining ½ teaspoon salt. Simmer, uncovered, until slightly thickened. Spoon sauce over chicken.   *Makes 4 servings*

Prep and cook time: 28 minutes

Serving Suggestion: Serve with a quick-cooking rice pilaf and mixed green salad.

Marinated Mustard Chicken

½ cup GREY POUPON® Dijon or COUNTRY DIJON® Mustard
½ teaspoon finely shredded orange peel
¼ cup orange juice
3 tablespoons vegetable oil
2 pounds meaty chicken pieces (breasts, thighs and drumsticks)
2 tablespoons honey

For marinade, in small bowl, whisk together mustard, orange peel, orange juice and oil until smooth. Rinse chicken; pat dry. In nonmetal dish, combine mustard mixture and chicken. Cover; chill for 6 to 24 hours, turning chicken occasionally. Remove chicken from marinade, *reserving ⅓ cup* marinade in saucepan.

Grill or broil chicken 6 inches from heat source for 35 to 45 minutes or until chicken is tender and no longer pink, turning once. Meanwhile, stir honey into reserved marinade. Bring to boil; reduce heat and simmer for 10 minutes, stirring occasionally. Brush marinade on chicken frequently during the last 10 minutes of grilling.
          Makes 4 servings

Prep time: 10 minutes
Chilling time: 6 hours
Cooking time: 45 minutes

Broiled Chicken with Honeyed Onion Sauce

Grilled Chicken Pasta Toss

6 boneless, skinless chicken breast halves (about 1½ pounds)
1 bottle (12 ounces) LAWRY'S® Herb & Garlic Marinade with Lemon Juice, divided
2 tablespoons olive or vegetable oil
1½ cups broccoli florets and sliced stems
1 cup Chinese pea pods
1 cup diagonally sliced carrots
1 can (2¼ ounces) sliced pitted ripe olives, drained
8 ounces fettuccine or linguine pasta, cooked, drained and kept hot

Pierce chicken several times with a fork. In a large resealable plastic bag or shallow glass dish, combine chicken and 1 cup Herb & Garlic Marinade; seal bag or cover dish. Marinate in refrigerator at least 30 minutes. Grill chicken,* 5 inches from heat source, 5 to 7 minutes on each side or until no longer pink in center, brushing halfway through cooking time with additional 2 tablespoons marinade. Remove chicken from grill and slice. Cover and set aside. In medium skillet heat oil. Add broccoli, pea pods and carrots; sauté over medium-high heat until crisp-tender. In large bowl, combine sautéed vegetables, olives, hot pasta and chicken. Pour remaining marinade over pasta and toss gently to coat thoroughly. *Makes 4 to 6 servings*

*Chicken may be thinly sliced and sautéed instead of grilled.

Presentation: Sprinkle with chopped fresh parsley, if desired.

Santa Fe Grilled Chicken

Juice of 2 to 3 fresh limes (½ cup), divided
2 tablespoons vegetable oil, divided
1 package (about 3 pounds) PERDUE® Fresh Skinless Pick of the Chicken
Salt and black pepper to taste
1 cup fresh or frozen diced peaches
¼ cup finely chopped red onion
1 jalapeño pepper, seeded and minced
2 cloves garlic, minced
1 teaspoon ground cumin
Chili powder

In medium-sized bowl, combine 7 tablespoons lime juice and 1 tablespoon plus 1½ teaspoons oil. Add chicken, salt and pepper; cover and marinate in the refrigerator 2 to 4 hours. Meanwhile to prepare salsa, in small bowl, combine remaining 1 tablespoon lime juice and 1½ teaspoons oil, peaches, onion, jalapeño pepper, garlic and cumin.

Prepare outdoor grill or preheat broiler. Remove chicken from marinade. Sprinkle with chili powder and place on cooking surface of grill over medium-hot coals or on broiler pan. Grill or broil 6 to 8 inches from heat source, allowing 20 to 30 minutes for breasts and 30 to 40 minutes for thighs and drumsticks, turning occasionally. Serve grilled chicken with salsa.

Makes 4 to 5 servings

Grilled Chicken Pasta Toss

Grilled Rosemary Chicken

2 tablespoons lemon juice
2 tablespoons olive oil
2 cloves garlic, minced
2 tablespoons minced fresh rosemary
¼ teaspoon salt
4 boneless skinless chicken breast halves

1. Whisk together lemon juice, oil, garlic, rosemary and salt in small bowl. Pour into shallow glass dish. Add chicken, turning to coat both sides with lemon juice mixture. Cover and marinate in refrigerator 15 minutes, turning chicken once.

2. Grill chicken over medium-hot coals 5 to 6 minutes per side or until chicken is no longer pink in center.   *Makes 4 servings*

Prep and cook time: 30 minutes

Roast Chicken Florentine

1 PERDUE® Fresh Young Chicken (2½ to 4 pounds)
  Salt and black pepper to taste
⅓ cup extra-virgin olive oil, divided
3 sprigs fresh rosemary *or* 1 tablespoon dried rosemary leaves, divided
2 lemons, divided
10 cloves garlic, unpeeled
2 packages (10 ounces each) fresh spinach, stemmed, rinsed and dried

Preheat oven to 350°F. Remove giblets from chicken. Rinse chicken and pat dry with paper towels. Season cavity with salt, pepper, 1 tablespoon oil and 1 sprig rosemary. Add juice of half a lemon to cavity. Truss chicken and place in roasting pan. Squeeze juice from remaining 1½ lemons over chicken; season with salt and pepper and drizzle with 1 tablespoon olive oil. Add garlic cloves and remaining rosemary to pan. Roast chicken in oven 1 to 1¼ hours until meat thermometer inserted in thickest part of thigh registers 180°F and juices run clear; baste occasionally with pan juices.

Remove chicken to serving platter and keep warm. Strain pan juices and extract garlic pulp from skins by pressing cloves through strainer. Skim fat from pan juices; whisk remaining oil into juices. To serve, arrange spinach on platter. Place chicken on spinach and drizzle with warm garlic sauce from roasting pan. Carve chicken into serving pieces.   *Makes 4 to 5 servings*

Grilled Rosemary Chicken

Chicken Pesto Mozzarella

6 to 8 ounces uncooked linguine or
    corkscrew pasta
4 boneless skinless chicken breast halves
    Salt and pepper (optional)
1 tablespoon olive oil
1 can (14½ ounces) DEL MONTE®
    FreshCut™ Diced Tomatoes with Basil,
    Garlic & Oregano
½ medium onion, chopped
⅓ cup sliced pitted ripe olives
4 teaspoons pesto sauce,* divided
¼ cup (1 ounce) shredded skim-milk
    mozzarella cheese
    Hot cooked pasta (optional)

*Pesto sauce is available frozen or refrigerated at the supermarket.

Cook pasta according to package directions; drain. Meanwhile, season chicken with salt and pepper, if desired. In large skillet, brown chicken in oil over medium-high heat. Add tomatoes, onion and olives; bring to a boil. Reduce heat to medium; cover and cook 8 minutes. Remove cover; cook over medium-high heat about 8 minutes or until chicken is no longer pink in center. Spread 1 teaspoon pesto over each breast; top with cheese. Cook, covered, until cheese melts. Serve over pasta, if desired.

Makes 4 servings

Prep time: 10 minutes
Cook time: 25 minutes

Simple Marinated Chicken Breasts

2 teaspoons Dijon mustard
1 clove garlic, minced
½ teaspoon salt
½ teaspoon ground black pepper
⅛ teaspoon dried savory
⅛ teaspoon dried tarragon
2 tablespoons olive oil, divided
¼ cup dry white wine
4 boneless, skinless chicken breast halves
    (about 1½ pounds)
½ cup warm water
    Fresh thyme for garnish

Combine mustard, garlic, salt, pepper, savory, tarragon, 1 tablespoon oil and wine in small bowl. Place chicken in shallow dish; pour mixture over chicken, turning to coat. Cover; marinate in refrigerator overnight.

Heat remaining 1 tablespoon oil in large skillet over medium heat until hot. Add chicken, reserving marinade; cook 15 minutes or until brown and no longer pink in center, turning occasionally. Remove to warm platter. Place marinade and warm water in skillet. Bring to a boil; cook and stir about 3 minutes. Pour over chicken. Garnish with thyme. Serve immediately.

Makes 4 servings

Favorite recipe from **National Broiler Council**

Chicken Pesto Mozzarella

Southern Fried Chicken

2½ to 3 pounds frying chicken pieces
  WESSON® Vegetable Oil
2 cups self-rising flour
2 teaspoons salt
1 teaspoon pepper
1 teaspoon paprika
1 teaspoon onion powder
½ teaspoon ground sage
¼ teaspoon garlic powder
2 eggs beaten with 2 tablespoons water

Rinse chicken and pat dry; set aside. Fill a large deep-fry pot or electric skillet to no more than half its depth with Wesson Oil. Heat oil to 325°F to 350°F. In bag, combine flour and seasonings. Shake chicken, one piece at a time, in flour mixture until coated. Dip in egg mixture, then shake again in flour mixture until completely coated. Fry chicken, a few pieces at a time, skin side down, for 10 to 14 minutes. Turn and fry chicken 10 minutes, covered, then 3 to 5 minutes, uncovered, or until chicken is tender and juices run clear. Drain on paper towels. Let stand 7 minutes before serving.

Makes 4 to 6 servings

Dijon-Chicken Spirals

4 boneless, skinless chicken breast halves
  (1 pound)
1 cup chopped parsley
¼ cup GREY POUPON® Dijon or
  COUNTRY DIJON® Mustard
2 tablespoons grated Parmesan cheese
1 teaspoon dried basil leaves, crushed
2 cloves garlic, minced

Rinse chicken; pat dry. Place *each* breast half, boned side up, between 2 pieces of clear plastic wrap. Working from center to the edges, pound lightly with the flat side of a meat mallet to ¼-inch thickness. Remove plastic wrap.

In small bowl, blend parsley, mustard, cheese, basil and garlic. Spread parsley mixture evenly on chicken breasts. Starting at short end, roll up each breast; cut each roll crosswise into 4 equal spirals. Arrange spirals on four 12-inch skewers.

Grill or broil skewers 6 inches from heat source for 10 to 15 minutes or until chicken is tender and no longer pink, turning once.

Makes 4 servings

Prep time: 20 minutes
Cooking time: 15 minutes

Southern Fried Chicken

Chicken with Orange and Basil

4 boneless skinless chicken breast halves
  (about 1½ pounds)
¾ cup fresh orange juice
½ cup dry white wine
2 tablespoons orange peel strips
½ cup sliced red onion
1 can (6 ounces) mandarin oranges, drained
¼ cup chopped fresh basil leaves *or* 2
  teaspoons dried basil leaves
Crumbled blue cheese (optional)

GRILL chicken on covered grill, over medium-hot coals 10 to 15 minutes or until chicken is no longer pink in center. Transfer to serving plate; keep warm.

COMBINE orange juice, wine and orange peel in same skillet; bring to a boil. Boil 5 minutes. Stir in onion; cook and stir about 5 minutes more or until onion is tender and sauce is reduced to about ¼ cup. Reduce heat; stir in oranges and basil. Spoon sauce over chicken; sprinkle with blue cheese, if desired.   *Makes 4 servings*

Serving Suggestion: Serve with a mixed green salad and sourdough rolls.

Roast Chicken Spanish Style

1 (4½- to 5-pound) whole roasting chicken
  Salt and freshly ground black pepper
1 clove garlic, cut in half
1 tablespoon FILIPPO BERIO® Olive Oil
½ teaspoon dried oregano leaves
1 medium onion, sliced
4 plum tomatoes, diced
2 medium green bell peppers, seeded and cut
  into chunks
1 (10-ounce) package whole mushrooms,
  cleaned and trimmed

Preheat oven to 450°F. Remove and discard giblets and neck from chicken. Rinse chicken under cold water; drain well and pat dry with paper towels. Sprinkle inside and outside of chicken with salt and black pepper. Rub outside of chicken with garlic. In small bowl, combine olive oil and oregano; brush over outside of chicken. Place chicken, breast side up, in shallow roasting pan. Roast 30 minutes or until skin is browned. *Reduce oven temperature to 375°F.* Add onion and tomatoes to pan. Cover pan with foil; bake an additional 1 hour to 1 hour and 15 minutes or until legs move freely and juices run clear, adding bell peppers and mushrooms about 20 minutes before chicken is done. Let stand 10 minutes before carving.   *Makes 6 servings*

Chicken with Orange and Basil

Chicken Primavera

4 boneless skinless chicken breast halves
3 tablespoons all-purpose flour
½ teaspoon dried basil leaves
¼ teaspoon salt
¼ teaspoon black pepper
1 package (16 ounces) frozen vegetable
   mixture (broccoli, red pepper, onion and
   mushroom combination)
4 teaspoons olive oil
2 cloves garlic, crushed
1 container (10 ounces) Alfredo sauce

1. Pound chicken breasts between 2 pieces of plastic wrap to ½-inch thickness with flat side of meat mallet or rolling pin. Combine flour, basil, salt and pepper in resealable plastic food storage bag. Add chicken; seal bag and shake to coat evenly with flour mixture. Set aside.

2. Make small cut in frozen vegetable package. Microwave at HIGH 2 minutes. Set aside.

3. Meanwhile, heat oil in large skillet over medium-high heat until hot. Add garlic; cook and stir 1 minute. Add chicken; cook 3 minutes per side. Reduce heat to medium.

4. Add vegetable mixture to skillet. Cook, covered, 5 to 8 minutes or until chicken is no longer pink in center and vegetables are tender.

5. Meanwhile, heat Alfredo sauce according to package directions. Spoon sauce over chicken and vegetables.   *Makes 4 servings*

Prep and cook time: 28 minutes

Serving Suggestion: Top with grated Parmesan cheese and serve with buttered spaghetti, tossed salad greens with Italian or Caesar salad dressing, breadsticks and a fresh fruit tart for dessert.

Almond Crusted Chicken Breasts

1½ cups BLUE DIAMOND® Sliced Natural
   Almonds, lightly toasted
2 whole chicken breasts, skinned, boned and
   cut in half
Salt
Pepper
¼ cup flour
1 egg, beaten with 2 teaspoons water
¼ cup butter, melted
1 teaspoon lemon juice
1½ teaspoons chopped fresh basil *or*
   ½ teaspoon dried basil

With hands, lightly crush almonds into small pieces; reserve. Lightly flatten chicken breasts. Season with salt and pepper. Dredge chicken in flour. Pat off excess flour. Dip chicken in beaten egg. Press each chicken breast in almonds, covering chicken well. Place on buttered baking sheet. Bake at 425°F. for 10 to 15 minutes or until chicken is just firm and no longer pink in center, and almonds are golden. Meanwhile, combine butter, lemon juice and basil. Drizzle over cooked chicken breasts.   *Makes 4 servings*

Chicken Primavera

Buffalo Chicken Drumsticks

8 large chicken drumsticks (about 2 pounds)
3 tablespoons hot pepper sauce
1 tablespoon vegetable oil
1 clove garlic, minced
¼ cup mayonnaise
3 tablespoons sour cream
1 tablespoon plus 1½ teaspoons white wine vinegar
¼ teaspoon sugar
⅓ cup (1½ ounces) crumbled Roquefort or blue cheese
2 cups hickory chips
Celery sticks

Place chicken in large resealable plastic food storage bag. Combine pepper sauce, oil and garlic in small bowl; pour over chicken. Seal bag tightly; turn to coat. Marinate in refrigerator at least 1 hour or, for hotter flavor, up to 24 hours, turning occasionally.

For blue cheese dressing, combine mayonnaise, sour cream, vinegar and sugar in another small bowl. Stir in cheese; cover and refrigerate until serving.

Prepare grill. Meanwhile, cover hickory chips with cold water; soak 20 minutes. Drain chicken, discarding marinade. Drain hickory chips; sprinkle over coals. Place chicken on grid. Grill, on covered grill, over medium-hot coals 25 to 30 minutes or until chicken is tender when pierced with fork and no longer pink near bone, turning 3 to 4 times. Serve with blue cheese dressing and celery sticks. *Makes 4 servings*

Hoisin Chicken Breast Supreme

½ cup hoisin sauce
3 tablespoons rice wine or sake
2 tablespoons sugar
2 tablespoons minced garlic
2 tablespoons reduced-sodium soy sauce
2 tablespoons ketchup
2½ pounds boneless skinless chicken breast halves

To prepare marinade, combine hoisin sauce, wine, sugar, garlic, soy sauce and ketchup in bowl. Add chicken and toss lightly to coat. Cover with plastic wrap and marinate in refrigerator several hours.

Preheat oven to 375°F. Remove chicken from marinade; discard marinade. Arrange chicken in baking pan lined with foil. Bake for 20 to 25 minutes or until no longer pink in center. Transfer to a platter and serve whole or cut into strips. *Makes 8 servings*

Note: To prepare in wok, cut chicken into strips before marinating. Heat 1 teaspoon vegetable oil in wok until hot. Add chicken and stir-fry until no longer pink.

Favorite recipe from **The Sugar Association, Inc.**

Chicken Cordon Bleu

6 boneless skinless chicken breast halves
    (1¼ pounds)
1 tablespoon Dijon-style mustard
3 slices (1 ounce each) lean ham, cut into
    halves
3 slices (1 ounce each) reduced-fat Swiss
    cheese, cut into halves
    Nonstick cooking spray
¼ cup unseasoned dry bread crumbs
2 tablespoons minced fresh parsley
3 cups hot cooked rice

Preheat oven to 350°F. Place chicken between 2 pieces of waxed paper; pound to ¼-inch thickness using flat side of meat mallet or rolling pin. Brush mustard on 1 side of each chicken breast; layer 1 slice each of ham and cheese over mustard. Roll up each chicken breast from short end; secure with wooden picks. Spray tops of chicken rolls with cooking spray; sprinkle with bread crumbs. Arrange chicken rolls in 11×7-inch baking pan. Cover; bake 10 minutes. Uncover; bake about 20 minutes or until chicken is no longer pink in center. Stir parsley into rice; serve with chicken. Serve with vegetables, if desired.

Makes 6 servings

Grilled Chicken with Pesto Sauce

⅓ cup olive oil
⅓ cup loosely packed parsley sprigs
⅓ cup GREY POUPON® Dijon or
    COUNTRY DIJON® Mustard
⅓ cup pine nuts or pignolia
2 tablespoons grated Parmesan cheese
2 cloves garlic
1 teaspoon dried basil leaves
6 boneless, skinless chicken thighs
    (1 pound)

For pesto sauce, in blender or food processor, blend oil, parsley, mustard, nuts, cheese, garlic and basil until combined. Reserve ½ *cup*.

Rinse chicken; pat dry. Grill or broil chicken 6 inches from heat source for 15 to 20 minutes or until chicken is tender and no longer pink, turning once. Brush frequently with remaining pesto sauce during last 10 minutes of grilling. Serve with reserved pesto sauce.

Makes 6 servings

Prep time: 10 minutes
Cooking time: 20 minutes

Chicken Cordon Bleu

Jamaican Rum Chicken

½ cup dark rum
2 tablespoons lime juice or lemon juice
2 tablespoons soy sauce
2 tablespoons brown sugar
4 large cloves garlic, minced
1 to 2 jalapeño peppers, seeded and minced*
1 tablespoon minced fresh ginger
1 teaspoon dried thyme leaves, crushed
½ teaspoon black pepper
6 boneless skinless chicken breast halves

*Jalapeño peppers sting and irritate skin. Wear rubber gloves when handling peppers and do not touch eyes. Wash hands after handling.

1. To prepare marinade, combine rum, lime juice, soy sauce, sugar, garlic, jalapeño peppers, ginger, thyme and black pepper in 2-quart glass measuring cup.

2. Rinse chicken and pat dry with paper towels. Place chicken in resealable plastic food storage bag. Pour marinade over chicken. Press air out of bag and seal tightly. Turn bag over to completely coat chicken with marinade. Refrigerate 4 hours or overnight, turning bag once or twice.

3. Prepare barbecue grill for direct grilling.

4. Drain chicken; reserve marinade. Grill chicken, on uncovered grill, over medium-hot coals 6 minutes per side or until chicken is no longer pink in center.

5. Meanwhile, bring remaining marinade to a boil in small saucepan over medium-high heat. Boil 5 minutes or until marinade is reduced by about half.

6. To serve, drizzle marinade over chicken. Garnish as desired.   *Makes 6 servings*

Cornmeal-Crusted Drums

¾ cup buttermilk
¼ cup finely chopped onion
1 package (about 1¼ pounds) PERDUE®
    Fresh Skinless Chicken Drumsticks
½ cup yellow cornmeal
½ cup fresh bread crumbs, lightly toasted
¼ cup grated Parmesan cheese
1 tablespoon chopped fresh thyme *or*
    1½ teaspoons dried thyme leaves
Dash ground red pepper
Salt and ground black pepper to taste
1 to 2 tablespoons vegetable oil

In medium bowl, combine buttermilk and onion. Add chicken; cover and marinate in refrigerator 2 to 3 hours.

Preheat oven to 425°F. On plate, combine cornmeal, bread crumbs, cheese, thyme, red pepper, salt and black pepper. Dredge chicken in crumbs, coating all sides. Place chicken on baking sheet; drizzle with oil. Bake 20 to 30 minutes until chicken is crisp and cooked through.   *Makes 2 to 3 servings*

Jamaican Rum Chicken

Apple-Stuffed Chicken

1 roasting chicken (4 to 5 pounds), giblets
    removed
½ teaspoon salt
½ teaspoon freshly ground black pepper
1 large Granny Smith apple, peeled, cored
    and thinly sliced
1 cup slivered yellow onion
6 ounces (1 carton) ALPINE LACE® Fat
    Free Cream Cheese with Garlic &
    Herbs
8 sprigs parsley, 6 inches long
1 sprig fresh rosemary, 5 inches long
¼ cup fresh lemon juice
2 tablespoons unsalted butter substitute

1. Preheat the oven to 425°F. Spray a large roasting pan and its rack with nonstick cooking spray. Rinse the chicken and pat dry with paper towels. Season the body and neck cavities of the chicken with the salt and pepper. In a small bowl, toss the apple and onion.

2. Gently loosen the skin of the chicken from the breast and spread the cream cheese between the skin and the breast meat. Stuff half of the apple-onion mixture under the skin.

3. Stuff the remaining apple-onion mixture into the body and neck cavities. Place the parsley and rosemary sprigs in the body cavity. Using cotton kitchen string, truss the chicken. Place the chicken on the rack, breast side up, in the roasting pan.

4. In a small saucepan, whisk the lemon juice and butter over medium heat until melted. Brush on the chicken. Roast for 45 minutes or until golden brown.

5. Reduce the oven temperature to 350°F and continue to roast, basting frequently with the pan drippings, for 1 hour or until the leg moves freely in its socket and/or a meat thermometer inserted in the thigh registers 180°F. Let the chicken stand for 10 minutes, discard the strings and remove the stuffing to a serving bowl.

6. Carve the chicken, discarding the skin but leaving the apple-onion layer beneath the skin. Discard the parsley and rosemary sprigs. Serve with the apple-onion stuffing and garnish with sprigs of fresh herbs, if you wish.

Makes 8 servings

Gingered Chicken Thighs

1 tablespoon peanut or vegetable oil
½ teaspoon hot chili oil
8 chicken thighs (1½ to 2 pounds)
2 cloves garlic, minced
¼ cup sweet and sour sauce
1 tablespoon soy sauce
2 teaspoons minced fresh ginger
  Cilantro and orange peel for garnish

Heat large, nonstick skillet over medium-high heat until hot. Add peanut oil and chili oil; heat until hot. Cook chicken thighs, skin side down, in hot oil 4 minutes or until golden brown. Reduce heat to low; turn chicken over. Cover, cook 15 to 18 minutes or until juices run clear. Spoon off fat.

Increase heat to medium. Cook and stir garlic 2 minutes. Combine sweet and sour sauce, soy sauce and ginger in small bowl. Brush half of mixture over chicken; turn chicken over and brush with remaining mixture. Cook 5 minutes, turning once more, until sauce has thickened and chicken is tender. Transfer chicken to serving platter; pour sauce evenly over chicken. Garnish with cilantro and orange peel.

Makes 4 servings

Chicken Breasts with Orange-Lime Sauce

2 whole chicken breasts, skinned, boned and
  cut in half
  Salt
  White pepper
7 tablespoons butter, divided
1 cup orange juice
1 tablespoon lime juice
¼ teaspoon grated orange peel
⅔ cup BLUE DIAMOND® Sliced Natural
  Almonds, toasted

Lightly flatten chicken breasts. Season with salt and pepper. Sauté breasts in 1 tablespoon melted butter in medium skillet for 2 to 3 minutes on each side or until no longer pink in center. Remove and keep warm. Add orange juice, lime juice and orange peel to skillet. Heat over high heat until mixture thickens to syrupy consistency. Add ½ teaspoon salt and ⅛ teaspoon pepper. Over low heat, whisk in remaining 6 tablespoons butter until sauce is thick and glossy. Add almonds and pour sauce over chicken.

Makes 4 servings

Gingered Chicken Thighs

Grilled Chicken with Orange-Cilantro Salsa

1 cup (11-ounce can) mandarin oranges, drained, ¼ cup juice reserved
1 cup coarsely chopped fresh cilantro
½ cup sliced red onion
¼ cup olive oil
¼ cup red wine vinegar
1 tablespoon ORTEGA® Diced Jalapeños
1 teaspoon salt
1 pound (3 to 4) boneless, skinless chicken breast halves

COMBINE oranges with reserved juice, cilantro, onion, oil, vinegar, jalapeños and salt in medium bowl; cover. Chill for at least 2 hours.

GRILL chicken over hot coals in barbecue, turning frequently, for 15 to 20 minutes or until chicken is no longer pink in center. Or, broil chicken in preheated broiler 4 to 5 inches from heat source, turning frequently, for 6 to 8 minutes or until chicken is no longer pink in center. Top each breast with salsa.   *Makes 4 servings*

Chicken Santa Fe

½ cup (2 ounces) shredded Monterey Jack cheese
½ cup (4-ounce can) ORTEGA® Diced Green Chiles
4 slices bacon
1 pound (3 to 4) boneless, skinless chicken breast halves
 ORTEGA® Thick & Chunky Salsa, mild
 Sliced avocados
 Chopped green onions

COMBINE cheese and chiles in medium bowl.

COOK bacon in large skillet over medium-high heat until crisp. Crumble bacon; add to cheese mixture. Discard all but 2 tablespoons drippings from skillet.

ADD chicken; cook, turning frequently, for 15 to 20 minutes or until no longer pink in center. Top each breast with ¼ cup cheese mixture; cover. Cook for 1 to 2 minutes or until cheese is melted. Top with salsa, avocados and green onions.
        Makes 4 servings

Grilled Chicken with Orange-Cilantro Salsa

Country Chicken in Rich Onion Gravy

1 tablespoon plus 2 teaspoons CHEF PAUL PRUDHOMME'S Poultry Magic®, divided
8 (2½ ounces each) boneless, skinless chicken breasts
6 tablespoons unsalted butter or margarine, divided
2 cups chopped onion
⅓ cup all purpose flour
2 cups chicken stock or water, divided
¼ teaspoon salt
2 cups hot, cooked rice, optional

Sprinkle ½ teaspoon Poultry Magic evenly over each chicken breast. Set aside.

In a 10-inch, heavy skillet over high heat, melt 2 tablespoons butter. When butter sizzles, add onion. Cook, stirring occasionally, about 5 minutes, or until onion starts to brown. Turn heat down to medium and continue cooking, stirring frequently, about 5 to 6 minutes or until onion is caramelized (rich brown color). Remove from heat and transfer onion to another container. Set aside.

Return skillet to high heat and add 3 tablespoons butter. When butter starts to sizzle, dredge 4 seasoned chicken pieces with flour. Shaking off excess flour, lay them in single layer in skillet. Cook about 1½ minutes per side or until golden brown. Remove from skillet. Add remaining 1 tablespoon butter and repeat procedure with remaining chicken.

Stir 1 cup stock into drippings in skillet to deglaze, stirring and scraping until skillet bottom is clean. Stir in caramelized onion and return chicken to skillet. Stir in remaining stock, Poultry Magic and salt and bring to boil. Reduce heat and simmer, stirring occasionally, about 20 minutes or until sauce has thickened slightly and chicken is fork tender. Remove from heat and serve with hot, cooked rice.   *Makes 4 servings*

Serving Suggestion: Pour ½ cup of sauce on each serving plate, covering bottom of plate. Mound ½ cup rice in center and place 1 chicken piece on each side of rice.

Baked Barbecue Chicken

1 (3-pound) broiler-fryer, cut up
1 small onion, cut into slices
1½ cups ketchup
½ cup packed brown sugar
¼ cup Worcestershire sauce
2 tablespoons lemon juice
1 tablespoon liquid smoke

PREHEAT oven to 375°F. Place chicken in 13×9-inch baking dish coated with nonstick cooking spray. Arrange onion slices over top.

COMBINE ketchup, brown sugar, Worcestershire sauce, lemon juice and liquid smoke in small saucepan. Heat over medium heat 2 to 3 minutes or until sugar dissolves. Pour over chicken.

BAKE chicken 1 hour or until chicken is no longer pink in center. Discard onion slices. Let stand 10 minutes before serving.

Makes 6 servings

Note: To spice up this dish, purée 1 or 2 canned chipotle peppers in a food processor and add the purée to the ketchup mixture.

Cajun Chicken Burgers

1 pound fresh ground chicken
1 small onion, finely chopped
¼ cup chopped green or red bell pepper
3 green onions, minced
1 clove garlic, minced
1 teaspoon Worcestershire sauce
½ teaspoon TABASCO® pepper sauce
Ground black pepper

In medium bowl, combine chicken, chopped onion, bell pepper, green onions, garlic, Worcestershire sauce, TABASCO® sauce and black pepper. Form into 5 (3-inch-diameter) patties. Broil or grill 6 minutes; turn over and broil or grill an additional 4 to 6 minutes or until no longer pink in centers. Serve immediately.

Makes 5 servings

Grilled Marinated Chicken

8 whole chicken legs (thighs and drumsticks attached) (about 3½ pounds)
6 ounces frozen lemonade concentrate, thawed
2 tablespoons white wine vinegar
1 tablespoon grated lemon peel
2 cloves garlic, minced

1. Remove skin and all visible fat from chicken. Place chicken in 13×9-inch glass baking dish. Combine remaining ingredients in small bowl; blend well. Pour over chicken; turn to coat. Cover; refrigerate 3 hours or overnight, turning occasionally.

2. To prevent sticking, spray grid with nonstick cooking spray. Prepare coals for grilling.

3. Place chicken on grill 4 inches from medium-hot coals. Grill 20 to 30 minutes or until chicken is no longer pink in center, turning occasionally. (Do not overcook or chicken will be dry.) Garnish with curly endive and lemon peel strips, if desired. *Makes 8 servings*

Cherry-Glazed Chicken

1 (2½- to 3-pound) broiler-fryer chicken, cut up (or 6 chicken breast halves, skinned and boned)
½ cup milk
½ cup all-purpose flour
1 teaspoon dried thyme leaves
  Salt and pepper, to taste
1 to 2 tablespoons vegetable oil
1 can (16 ounces) unsweetened tart cherries
¼ cup granulated sugar
¼ cup brown sugar
1 teaspoon prepared yellow mustard

Rinse chicken; pat dry with paper towels. Pour milk into shallow container. In another container, combine flour, thyme, salt and pepper. Dip chicken first into milk, then into flour mixture; coat evenly.

Heat oil in large skillet. Add chicken; brown on all sides. Put chicken in 13×9×2-inch baking dish. Bake, covered with foil, in preheated 350°F oven 30 minutes.

Meanwhile, drain cherries, reserving ½ cup juice. In a saucepan, combine cherries, reserved cherry juice and sugars; mix well. Bring mixture to a boil over medium heat. Add mustard; mix well. Cook 5 minutes or until slightly thickened.

After chicken has cooked 30 minutes, remove baking dish from oven. Carefully remove foil; spoon hot cherry mixture evenly over chicken. Bake, uncovered, 15 minutes or until chicken is no longer pink in centers. Serve immediately. *Makes 6 servings*

Favorite recipe from **Cherry Marketing Institute, Inc.**

Grilled Marinated Chicken

Buttermilk Ranch Fried Chicken

2½ to 3 pounds frying chicken pieces
  WESSON® Vegetable Oil
2¼ cups all-purpose flour
1¼ tablespoons dried dill weed
1½ teaspoons salt
¾ teaspoon pepper
2½ cups buttermilk

Rinse chicken and pat dry; set aside. Fill a large deep-fry pot or electric skillet to no more than half its depth with Wesson Oil. Heat oil to 325°F to 350°F. In a medium bowl, combine flour, dill, salt and pepper. Fill another bowl with buttermilk. Place chicken, one piece at a time, in buttermilk; shake off excess liquid. Coat lightly in flour mixture; shake off excess flour. Dip once again in buttermilk and flour mixture. Fry chicken, a few pieces at a time, skin side down, for 10 to 14 minutes. Turn chicken and fry 12 to 15 minutes longer or until juices run clear; drain on paper towels. Let stand 7 minutes before serving.

Makes 4 to 6 servings

Chicken Pesto Tortelloni

1 package (7 ounces) DI GIORNO® Pesto
  Sauce
¼ cup KRAFT® Real Mayonnaise
4 boneless skinless chicken breast halves
  (about 1¼ pounds)
2 packages (9 ounces each) DI GIORNO®
  Pesto Tortelloni, cooked, drained
½ cup sliced pitted ripe olives
1 cup chopped seeded tomatoes

MIX pesto sauce and mayonnaise.

PLACE chicken on grill over medium-hot coals or rack of broiler pan. Grill or broil 7 minutes on each side or until tender and no longer pink in center, brushing with ¼ cup pesto mixture during the last 3 minutes of cooking time. Cut chicken into thin strips.

TOSS chicken with pasta, olives, tomatoes and remaining pesto mixture. Sprinkle with Parmesan cheese, if desired. Serve warm or chilled.

Makes about 6 servings

Note: Recipe may be halved. Prepare with ⅓ cup DI GIORNO® Pesto Sauce, ¼ cup KRAFT® Real Mayonnaise, 2 boneless skinless chicken breasts, 1 package DI GIORNO® Pesto Tortelloni, ¼ cup sliced pitted ripe olives and ½ cup chopped tomato.

Buttermilk Ranch Fried Chicken

Spicy Chicken Stromboli

1 cup frozen broccoli florets, thawed
1 can (10 ounces) diced chicken
1½ cups (6 ounces) shredded Monterey Jack
    cheese with jalapeño peppers
¼ cup chunky salsa
2 green onions, chopped
1 can (10 ounces) pizza crust dough

1. Preheat oven to 400°F. Coarsely chop broccoli. Combine broccoli, chicken, cheese, salsa and green onions in small bowl.

2. Unroll pizza dough. Pat into 15×10-inch rectangle. Sprinkle broccoli mixture evenly over top. Starting with long side, tightly roll into log jelly-roll style. Pinch seam to seal. Place on baking sheet, seam side down.

3. Bake 15 to 20 minutes or until golden brown. Transfer to wire rack to cool slightly. Slice and serve warm. *Makes 6 servings*

Prep and cook time: 30 minutes

Lemon Pepper Chicken

⅓ cup lemon juice
¼ cup olive oil
¼ cup finely chopped onion
3 cloves garlic, minced
1 tablespoon cracked black pepper
1 tablespoon brown sugar
2 teaspoons grated lemon peel
¾ teaspoon salt
4 chicken quarters (about 2½ pounds)

COMBINE lemon juice, oil, onion, garlic, pepper, brown sugar, lemon peel and salt in small bowl; reserve 2 tablespoons marinade. Combine remaining marinade and chicken in large resealable plastic food storage bag. Seal bag; knead to coat chicken. Refrigerate 4 hours or overnight.

REMOVE chicken from marinade; discard marinade. Arrange chicken on microwavable plate; cover with waxed paper. Microwave at HIGH 5 minutes. Turn and rearrange chicken. Cover and microwave at HIGH 5 minutes.

TRANSFER chicken to grill. Grill covered over medium-hot coals 15 to 20 minutes or until chicken is no longer pink in center and juices run clear, turning several times and basting with reserved marinade. *Makes 4 servings*

Serving Suggestion: Serve with a mixed green salad and fresh lemon slices.

Spicy Chicken Stromboli

Quick

MEALS FROM 6 INGREDIENTS

Chicken and Asparagus Stir-Fry

1 cup uncooked rice
2 tablespoons vegetable oil, divided
1 pound boneless skinless chicken breasts,
    cut into ½-inch-wide strips
2 medium red bell peppers, cut into thin
    strips
½ pound fresh asparagus, cut diagonally into
    1-inch pieces
½ cup bottled stir-fry sauce

1. Cook rice according to package directions.

2. Heat 1 tablespoon oil in wok or large skillet over medium-high heat until hot. Stir-fry chicken 3 to 4 minutes or until chicken is no longer pink. Remove from wok; set aside.

3. Heat remaining 1 tablespoon oil in wok until hot. Stir-fry bell peppers and asparagus 1 minute; reduce heat to medium. Cover and cook 2 minutes or until vegetables are crisp-tender, stirring once or twice.

4. Stir in chicken and sauce; heat through. Serve immediately with rice.   *Makes 4 servings*

Prep and cook time: 18 minutes

Chicken and Asparagus Stir-Fry

Country Herb Roasted Chicken

1 chicken (2½ to 3 pounds), cut into
  serving pieces (with or without skin) *or*
  1½ pounds boneless skinless chicken
  breast halves
1 envelope LIPTON® Recipe Secrets®
  Savory Herb with Garlic or Golden
  Herb with Lemon Soup Mix
2 tablespoons water
1 tablespoon olive or vegetable oil

Preheat oven to 375°F. In 13×9-inch baking or roasting pan, arrange chicken. In small bowl, combine remaining ingredients; brush on chicken.

For **chicken pieces,** bake uncovered 45 minutes or until chicken is no longer pink near bone. For **chicken breast halves,** bake uncovered 20 minutes or until no longer pink in center.

Makes about 4 servings

Menu Suggestions: Serve with a lettuce and tomato salad, scalloped potatoes and cooked green beans.

Chile Rellenos-Style Chicken

6 boneless skinless chicken breast halves
1 envelope SHAKE 'N BAKE® Seasoning
  and Coating Mixture—Hot & Spicy
  Recipe for Chicken or Pork
½ cup KRAFT® Natural Shredded
  Cheddar/Monterey Jack Cheese
1 can (4 ounces) chopped green chilies,
  drained

HEAT oven to 400°F.

COAT chicken with coating mixture as directed on package.

BAKE 20 minutes on ungreased or foil-lined baking pan. Mix cheese and chilies. Spoon over chicken. Bake 5 minutes or until chicken is cooked through and cheese is melted. Serve with salsa, if desired.

Makes 4 servings

Ready in: 25 minutes

Country Herb Roasted Chicken

Chicken Parmesan Noodle Bake

1 package (12 ounces) extra wide noodles
4 half boneless chicken breasts, skinned
½ teaspoon rosemary, crushed
2 cans (14½ ounces each) DEL MONTE®
   FreshCut™ Diced Tomatoes with Basil,
   Garlic and Oregano
½ cup (2 ounces) shredded mozzarella cheese
¼ cup (1 ounce) grated Parmesan cheese

1. Preheat oven to 450°F.

2. Cook noodles according to package directions; drain. Keep warm.

3. Meanwhile, sprinkle chicken with rosemary; season with salt and pepper, if desired. Arrange chicken in shallow baking dish. Bake, uncovered, 20 minutes or until chicken is no longer pink in center. Drain; remove chicken from dish.

4. Drain tomatoes, reserving liquid. In large bowl, toss reserved liquid with noodles; place in baking dish. Top with chicken and tomatoes. Sprinkle with cheeses.

5. Bake 10 minutes or until heated through. Sprinkle with additional Parmesan cheese and garnish, if desired.   *Makes 4 servings*

Prep & bake time: 35 minutes

Honey-Mustard Glazed Chicken

2 tablespoons Dijon-style mustard
2 tablespoons honey
1 tablespoon butter or margarine, melted
1 teaspoon MCCORMICK®/SCHILLING®
   Basil Leaves
½ teaspoon MCCORMICK®/SCHILLING®
   California Style Garlic Powder
1 pound boneless, skinless chicken breasts
   (4 half breasts)

1. Preheat broiler or grill.

2. Combine mustard, honey, butter, basil and garlic powder in small bowl and beat until well mixed.

3. Arrange chicken on lightly greased broiler pan or grill and broil 3 to 4 minutes. Brush half of mustard mixture on chicken and broil 2 minutes.

4. Turn chicken over and broil 3 to 4 minutes. Brush with remaining mustard mixture. Broil 2 minutes or until chicken is no longer pink in center.   *Makes 4 servings*

Chicken Parmesan Noodle Bake

Mustard-Glazed Chicken Sandwiches

½ cup honey-mustard barbecue sauce, divided
4 kaiser rolls, split
4 boneless skinless chicken breast halves (about 1 pound)
4 slices Swiss cheese
4 leaves leaf lettuce
8 slices tomato

1. Spread about 1 teaspoon barbecue sauce on cut sides of each roll.

2. Pound chicken breast halves between 2 pieces of plastic wrap to ½-inch thickness with flat side of meat mallet or rolling pin. Spread remaining barbecue sauce over chicken.

3. Cook chicken in large nonstick skillet over medium-low heat 5 minutes per side or until no longer pink in center. Remove skillet from heat. Place cheese slices on chicken; let stand 3 minutes to melt.

4. Place lettuce leaves and tomato slices on roll bottoms; top with chicken and roll tops.

Makes 4 servings

Prep and cook time: 19 minutes

Serving Suggestion: Serve sandwiches with yellow pear tomatoes, baby carrots and celery sticks.

Spanish Skillet Supper

1 tablespoon vegetable oil
1 pound boneless skinless chicken breasts, cut into 1-inch cubes
2 cups hot water
1 package (4.4 ounces) Spanish rice and sauce mix
2 cups BIRDS EYE® frozen green peas
Crushed red pepper flakes

• Heat oil in large skillet over medium-high heat. Add chicken; cook and stir until lightly browned, about 5 minutes.

• Add hot water and rice and sauce mix; bring to boil. Reduce heat to medium-low; simmer, uncovered, 5 minutes.

• Stir in green peas; increase heat to medium-high. Cover and cook 5 minutes or until peas and rice are tender.

• Sprinkle with red pepper flakes.

Makes about 4 servings

Prep time: 5 minutes
Cook time: 20 minutes

Mustard-Glazed Chicken Sandwich

Chicken-Pesto Pizza

8 ounces chicken tenders
1 medium onion, thinly sliced
⅓ cup prepared pesto
3 medium plum tomatoes, thinly sliced
1 (14-inch) prepared pizza crust
1 cup (4 ounces) shredded mozzarella cheese

1. Preheat oven to 450°F. Cut chicken tenders into bite-size pieces. Coat medium nonstick skillet with nonstick cooking spray; cook and stir chicken over medium heat 2 minutes. Add onion and pesto; cook and stir about 3 minutes or until chicken is no longer pink.

2. Arrange tomato slices and chicken mixture on pizza crust to within 1 inch of edge. Sprinkle cheese over top. Bake 8 minutes or until pizza is hot and cheese is melted and bubbly.

Makes 6 servings

Prep and cook time: 22 minutes

Crispy Ranch Chicken

1½ cups cornflake crumbs
1 teaspoon dried rosemary leaves
½ teaspoon salt
½ teaspoon fresh ground black pepper
1½ cups ranch salad dressing
3 pounds chicken pieces

PREHEAT oven to 375°F. Combine cornflake crumbs, rosemary, salt and pepper in medium bowl.

POUR salad dressing into separate medium bowl. Dip chicken pieces in salad dressing, coating well. Dredge coated chicken in crumb mixture.

PLACE in 13 X 9-inch baking dish coated with nonstick cooking spray. Bake 50 to 55 minutes or until chicken is no longer pink in center and juices run clear.

Makes 6 servings

Serving Suggestion: Serve with peas and carrots and creamy mashed potatoes.

Chicken-Pesto Pizza

All-American Barbecued Roaster

1 PERDUE® OVEN STUFFER® roaster
  (6 to 8 pounds)
  Salt
  Pepper
1 cup vegetable oil
⅓ cup red wine vinegar
1 teaspoon paprika

Preheat gas grill following manufacturer's directions. Or, prepare charcoal grill for indirect cooking, arranging coals on each side of rectangular metal or foil drip pan. Add mesquite or hickory chunks or chips, if desired, for additional smoky flavor.

Remove giblets from roaster; reserve for other uses. Rinse roaster under cold running water; pat dry with paper towels. Sprinkle salt and pepper inside cavity and over outside of roaster, if desired. Tuck wings under back; tie legs together with wet kitchen string.

To prepare basting sauce, in small bowl, combine oil, vinegar, paprika, 2 teaspoons salt and ½ teaspoon pepper; whisk until well combined and thickened. Place roaster, breast side up, on grid directly over drip pan. Grill roaster, covered, about 2 hours. After first 30 minutes, brush with basting sauce. Continue to grill, covered, brushing with basting sauce every 15 minutes. Begin

checking for doneness after 1½ hours; roaster is done if BIRD WATCHER® thermometer pops up, legs move freely and juices run clear. A meat thermometer also should register 180°F when inserted in the thickest part of the thigh. If necessary, wrap small pieces of foil around wings and drumsticks to prevent burning.

Makes 6 servings

International Basting Sauce Variations:

Italian Roaster: Prepare basting sauce as directed, adding 1 cup ketchup, 2 cloves minced garlic, 1 teaspoon dried oregano leaves and ½ teaspoon dried basil leaves to sauce.

French Roaster: Prepare basting sauce as directed, adding ⅓ cup minced shallots, ⅓ cup Dijon-style mustard and 1 teaspoon dried tarragon leaves to sauce.

German Roaster: Prepare basting sauce as directed, adding ½ cup beer, 2 tablespoons molasses and 2 tablespoons caraway seeds to sauce.

Chinese Roaster: Prepare basting sauce as directed, adding ⅓ cup soy sauce, 2 cloves minced garlic and 1 tablespoon grated fresh ginger *or* 1 teaspoon ground ginger to sauce.

Lemon-Herb Chicken

1 egg
½ cup dry bread crumbs
1½ teaspoons MCCORMICK®/SCHILLING®
    Lemon & Pepper Seasoning
1 pound boneless, skinless chicken breasts
    (4 half breasts)
2 tablespoons vegetable oil

1. Place egg in pie plate and beat lightly. Place bread crumbs on large piece of wax paper. Add seasoning. Stir with fork until well combined.

2. Dip chicken breasts, 1 at a time, in beaten egg. Allow excess egg to drip off. Coat chicken evenly in bread crumb mixture.

3. Heat oil in skillet. Add coated chicken and sauté 5 to 6 minutes. Turn chicken over and cook 5 to 6 minutes or until no longer pink in center. Drain on paper towels. *Makes 4 servings*

Minute® Easy Chicken Stir-Fry

2 pouches MINUTE® Boil-in-Bag Rice,
    uncooked
1 tablespoon oil
4 boneless skinless chicken breast halves
    (about 1¼ pounds), cut into strips
3 cups fresh or frozen stir-fry vegetables,
    thawed
¾ cup bottled stir-fry sauce

PREPARE rice as directed on package

HEAT oil in nonstick skillet. Add chicken; cook and stir 5 minutes. Add vegetables and sauce; cover.

SIMMER on low heat 4 minutes. Serve over rice.
Makes 4 servings

Prep time: 5 minutes
Cook time: 10 minutes

Honey Roasted Chicken

3 tablespoons FILIPPO BERIO® Olive Oil
2 tablespoons orange juice
2 tablespoons honey
1¼ teaspoons paprika
2½ pounds chicken quarters

Preheat oven to 425°F. In small bowl, whisk together olive oil, orange juice, honey and paprika. Brush chicken pieces generously with olive oil mixture. Arrange chicken in roasting pan. Roast 15 minutes. *Reduce oven temperature to 400°F.* Baste chicken again with olive oil mixture. Roast chicken, basting occasionally, 30 to 40 minutes or until chicken is no longer pink in center and juices run clear.
Makes 4 servings

Chicken and Asparagus Hollandaise

1 package (1.25 ounces) hollandaise sauce
   mix
1 pound boneless chicken breasts, cut into
   strips
2 teaspoons lemon juice
1 box (10 ounces) BIRDS EYE® frozen
   asparagus
   Dash cayenne pepper

• Prepare hollandaise sauce according to package directions.

• Spray large skillet with nonstick cooking spray; cook chicken strips over medium-high heat 10 to 12 minutes or until browned, stirring occasionally.

• Add hollandaise sauce, lemon juice and asparagus.

• Cover and cook, stirring occasionally, 5 to 10 minutes or until asparagus is heated through. (*Do not overcook.*)

• Add cayenne pepper and salt and black pepper to taste.   *Makes 4 to 6 servings*

Prep time: 10 minutes

Cook time: 20 to 25 minutes

Serving Suggestion: Serve over rice or noodles.

Barbecued Orange Chicken

1 cup KRAFT® Thick 'N Spicy Barbecue
   Sauce with Honey or KRAFT® Original
   Barbecue Sauce
¼ cup orange juice
1 tablespoon grated orange peel
3 pound broiler-fryer chicken, quartered *or*
   2 large Cornish game hens, split
   Orange slices, for garnish

COMBINE barbecue sauce, orange juice and peel in heavy plastic bag or glass baking dish. Add chicken to sauce; turn to coat well. Close bag or cover dish and let stand at room temperature 30 minutes or refrigerate until ready to cook.

PREHEAT oven to 400°F. Remove chicken from barbecue sauce; reserving sauce. Place chicken, skin side up, on rack in foil-lined roasting pan. Bake 40 to 50 minutes or until chicken is cooked through, basting with reserved sauce three times. Garnish with orange slices.   *Makes 4 servings*

Ready in: 50 minutes

Chicken and Asparagus Hollandaise

Honey-Lime Glazed Chicken

1 whole chicken, quartered (about
    3 pounds) or 3 pounds chicken pieces
⅓ cup honey
2 tablespoons fresh lime juice
1 tablespoon plus 1½ teaspoons reduced-
    sodium soy sauce
3 cups hot, cooked noodles (3½ ounces
    uncooked)

1. Preheat oven to 375°F. Arrange chicken, skin side up, in single layer in shallow casserole dish or 11×7-inch baking dish.

2. Combine remaining ingredients except noodles in small bowl; blend well. Brush one third of honey mixture over chicken; bake 15 minutes.

3. Brush remaining honey mixture over chicken; bake 10 to 15 minutes more or until no longer pink in center and juices run clear. Serve with noodles.   *Makes 4 servings*

Chicky Quicky

1 cup SONOMA Dried Tomato Bits®
8 chicken thighs (or breast halves)
    Juice of 1 lemon
1 tablespoon rosemary
    Salt and pepper, to taste

Place tomato bits in bottom of baking pan; arrange chicken in one layer on top of tomatoes. Squeeze lemon juice over chicken. Sprinkle rosemary, salt and pepper over chicken.

Cover and bake at 350°F until tender, about 40 to 45 minutes. Before serving, spoon juices over top of chicken.   *Makes 4 servings*

Lemon Basil Chicken

1 cup MIRACLE WHIP® Salad Dressing
2 tablespoons fresh lemon juice
2 teaspoons honey
1 teaspoon dried basil leaves
1 broiler-fryer chicken (2½ to 3 pounds),
    cut up

HEAT oven to 375°F.

MIX salad dressing, juice, honey and basil. Place chicken in 13×9-inch baking dish. Spread with salad dressing mixture.

BAKE 45 minutes or until chicken is cooked through.   *Makes 4 servings*

Ready in: 45 minutes

Honey-Lime Glazed Chicken

Peppy Pesto Toss

8 ounces uncooked ziti or mostaccioli
1 package (16 ounces) frozen bell pepper and onion strips, thawed
½ pound deli chicken breast or smoked chicken breast, cut ½ inch thick
1 cup half-and-half
½ cup pesto sauce
¼ cup grated or shaved Parmesan or Asiago cheese

1. Cook pasta according to package directions, adding pepper and onion mixture to pasta water during last 2 minutes of cooking.

2. Meanwhile, cut chicken into ½-inch cubes.

3. Drain pasta and vegetables in colander.

4. Combine half-and-half, pesto and chicken in saucepan used to prepare pasta. Cook 2 minutes or until heated through. Return pasta and vegetables to saucepan; toss well.

5. Sprinkle with cheese. Serve immediately.
Makes 4 servings

Prep and cook time: 20 minutes

Chicken Cacciatore

1 pound boneless chicken breasts, cut into strips
1 bag (16 ounces) BIRDS EYE® frozen Farm Fresh Mixtures Broccoli, Cauliflower and Carrots
1 jar (14 ounces) prepared spaghetti sauce
½ cup sliced black olives
¼ cup water
¼ cup grated Parmesan cheese

• Spray large skillet with nonstick cooking spray; cook chicken over medium heat 7 to 10 minutes or until browned, stirring occasionally.

• Add vegetables, spaghetti sauce, olives and water. Cover and cook 10 to 15 minutes or until vegetables are heated through.

• Sprinkle cheese over top before serving. Add salt, pepper and/or garlic powder to taste.
Makes 4 to 6 servings

Prep time: 5 to 10 minutes
Cook time: 20 to 25 minutes

Reuben Chicken Melts

  4 boneless skinless chicken breast halves
  1 large onion, cut into ½-inch slices
  1¼ cups Thousand Island salad dressing, divided
  2 cups shredded red cabbage
  1½ cups (6 ounces) shredded Swiss cheese
  4 French rolls, split

1. Brush chicken and onion with ½ cup salad dressing; set aside.

2. Combine ¼ cup salad dressing and cabbage; mix well. Set aside.

3. Grill chicken over hot coals 5 to 7 minutes on each side or until no longer pink in center. Sprinkle chicken evenly with Swiss cheese during last minute of grilling. Grill onion 4 to 5 minutes on each side or until browned and tender. Grill rolls until toasted.

4. Spread toasted sides of rolls with remaining ½ cup salad dressing. Place chicken on roll bottoms. Top with onion, cabbage mixture and roll tops.

Makes 4 servings

Prep and cook time: 25 minutes

Apricot Glazed Chicken

  ½ cup WISH-BONE® Italian Dressing
  2 teaspoons ground ginger (optional)
  1 (2½- to 3-pound) chicken, cut into serving pieces
  ¼ cup apricot or peach preserves

In large, shallow nonaluminum baking dish or plastic bag, blend Italian dressing and ginger. Add chicken; turn to coat. Cover, or close bag, and marinate in refrigerator, turning occasionally, 3 to 24 hours.

Remove chicken from marinade, reserving ¼ cup marinade. In small saucepan, bring reserved marinade to a boil and continue boiling 1 minute. Remove from heat and stir in preserves until melted; set aside.

Grill or broil chicken until chicken is no longer pink in center, brushing with preserves mixture during last 5 minutes of cooking.

Makes 4 servings

Note: Also terrific with WISH-BONE® Robusto Italian Dressing.

Reuben Chicken Melt

Chicken Breasts Smothered in Tomatoes and Mozzarella

4 boneless skinless chicken breast halves (about 1½ pounds)
3 tablespoons olive oil, divided
1 cup chopped onions
2 teaspoons bottled minced garlic
1 can (14½ ounces) Italian-style stewed tomatoes
1½ cups (6 ounces) shredded mozzarella cheese

1. Preheat broiler.

2. Pound chicken breasts between 2 pieces of plastic wrap to ¼-inch thickness using flat side of meat mallet or rolling pin.

3. Heat 2 tablespoons oil in ovenproof skillet over medium heat. Add chicken and cook 3 to 4 minutes per side or until no longer pink in center. Transfer to plate; cover and keep warm.

4. Heat remaining 1 tablespoon oil in same skillet over medium heat. Add onions and garlic; cook and stir 3 minutes. Add tomatoes; bring to a simmer. Return chicken to skillet, spooning tomato mixture over chicken.

5. Sprinkle cheese over top. Broil 4 to 5 inches from heat source until cheese is melted.

Makes 4 servings

Prep and cook time: 20 minutes

Quick-as-a-Wink Chicken

1 package (about 2¼ pounds) PERDUE® Fresh Skinless Split Chicken Breasts
Salt and ground pepper to taste
½ cup prepared Italian salad dressing
2 cups hot cooked rice (optional)
2 tablespoons fresh minced parsley (optional)
Lemon wedges (optional)

Preheat oven to 350°F. Season chicken with salt and pepper; place in 12×8-inch baking dish. Pour salad dressing over chicken. Turn chicken to coat with dressing. Bake, uncovered, 10 minutes. Turn chicken and bake 15 minutes longer or until cooked through. To serve, place chicken over rice; sprinkle with parsley and garnish with lemon wedges.

Makes 4 servings

Prep time: about 5 minutes
Cook time: 25 minutes

Chicken Breast Smothered in Tomatoes and Mozzarella

Caesar Chicken Salad

1 envelope GOOD SEASONS® Gourmet
    Caesar Salad Dressing Mix
¼ cup lemon juice
1 pound boneless skinless chicken breast
    halves, cut into strips
6 cups torn romaine lettuce
1 cup croutons
½ cup (2 ounces) KRAFT® 100% Grated
    Parmesan Cheese

PREPARE salad dressing mix as directed on
envelope, except substitute lemon juice for
vinegar.

COOK chicken in 1 tablespoon of the prepared
dressing in skillet on medium heat until cooked
through.

PLACE lettuce, chicken, croutons and cheese in
large salad bowl. Add remaining dressing; toss to
coat well.   *Makes 4 servings*

Ready in: 10 minutes

One-Dish Chicken Bake

1 package (6 ounces) STOVE TOP®
    Stuffing Mix for Chicken
4 boneless skinless chicken breast halves
    (about 1¼ pounds)
1 can (10¾ ounces) condensed cream of
    mushroom soup
⅓ cup BREAKSTONE® or KNUDSEN®
    Sour Cream *or* milk

PREPARE stuffing mix as directed on package;
set aside.

PLACE chicken in 12×8-inch baking dish. Mix
soup and sour cream; pour over chicken. Top
with stuffing.

BAKE at 375°F for 35 minutes or until chicken
is cooked through.   *Makes 4 servings*

Prep time: 10 minutes
Bake time: 35 minutes

Grilled Ginger Chicken with Pineapple and Coconut Rice

1 can (20 ounces) pineapple rings in juice
1 cup uncooked white rice
½ cup sweetened flaked coconut
4 boneless skinless chicken breast halves
    (about 1¼ pounds)
1 tablespoon soy sauce
1 teaspoon ground ginger

1. Drain juice from pineapple into glass measure. Reserve 2 tablespoons juice for chicken. Combine remaining juice with enough water to equal 2 cups.

2. Cook and stir rice and coconut in medium saucepan over medium heat 3 to 4 minutes or until lightly browned. Add juice mixture; cover and bring to a boil. Reduce heat to low; cook 15 minutes or until rice is tender and liquid is absorbed.

3. While rice is cooking, combine chicken, reserved juice, soy sauce and ginger in medium bowl; toss well.

4. Grill or broil chicken 6 minutes; turn. Add pineapple rings to grill or broiler pan. Cook 6 to 8 minutes or until chicken is no longer pink in center, turning pineapple after 3 minutes.

5. Transfer rice to four serving plates; serve with chicken and pineapple.   *Makes 4 servings*

Prep and cook time: 22 minutes

Crispy Baked Chicken

8 ounces (1 cup) nonfat French onion dip
    Skim milk
1 cup cornflake crumbs
½ cup wheat germ
6 skinless chicken breast halves or thighs
    (about 1½ pounds)

1. Preheat oven to 350°F. Spray baking pan with nonstick cooking spray.

2. Place dip in shallow bowl; stir until smooth. Add milk, 1 tablespoon at a time, until pourable consistency is reached.

3. Combine cornflake crumbs and wheat germ on plate.

4. Dip chicken pieces in milk mixture; then roll in corn flake mixture. Discard milk mixture. Place chicken in prepared pan. Bake 45 to 50 minutes or until juices run clear when pierced with fork and chicken is no longer pink in center.
Makes 6 servings

Grilled Ginger Chicken with Pineapple and Coconut Rice

Savory
LIGHT DINNERS

Barbecued Chicken Pizza

2 tablespoons yellow cornmeal
1 pound frozen bread dough, thawed
¾ cup hickory smoked barbecue sauce, divided
1½ cups (6 ounces) shredded ALPINE LACE® Fat Free Pasteurized Process Skim Milk Cheese Product—For Mozzarella Lovers, divided
2 tablespoons olive oil, divided
12 ounces boneless skinless chicken breasts, cut into 2½×½-inch strips
1 teaspoon minced garlic
¼ teaspoon salt, or to taste
¼ teaspoon crushed red pepper flakes
4 ounces mushrooms, sliced
1½ cups thin red bell pepper strips
3 green onion tops, cut into thin 1-inch strips

1. Preheat the oven to 425°F. Spray a 15-inch round pizza pan or a 15×10×1-inch baking pan with nonstick cooking spray and sprinkle with the cornmeal. Spray a large nonstick skillet with the cooking spray.

2. Gently press the bread dough onto the bottom and up the sides of the pan. Spread ½ cup of barbecue sauce evenly over the crust and sprinkle with ¾ cup of the mozzarella.

3. In the skillet, heat 1 tablespoon of the oil over medium-high heat. Add the chicken, garlic, salt and crushed red pepper flakes. Sauté for 4 minutes. Using a slotted spoon, transfer to a medium-size bowl; toss with the remaining ¼ cup of barbecue sauce. Arrange the chicken strips on the top of the pizza, then spoon over any sauce remaining in the bowl.

4. In the same skillet, heat the remaining tablespoon of oil. Add the mushrooms and bell pepper and sauté for 5 minutes; arrange on the pizza. Sprinkle with the remaining ¾ cup of mozzarella. Bake for 15 to 20 minutes or until the cheese melts. Sprinkle with the onion.

Makes 8 servings

Nutrients per Serving:

Calories: 293, Total Fat: 7 g, Cholesterol: 28 mg

Barbecued Chicken Pizza

Tex-Mex Chicken Kabobs

¾ cup barbecue sauce
¼ cup molasses
2 tablespoons orange juice
2 teaspoons chili powder
1 pound chicken tenders
1 cup (1-inch) red bell pepper pieces
1 cup (1-inch) onion pieces
1 cup (1-inch) zucchini pieces

1. Combine barbecue sauce, molasses, orange juice and chili powder in small bowl; stir to blend. (Sauce mixture can be covered and refrigerated up to 1 week before using, if desired.)

2. Reserve ⅔ cup sauce mixture for serving; set aside. Thread chicken and vegetables alternately on metal skewers. Grill or broil kabobs 15 to 18 minutes or until chicken is no longer pink in center, brushing with remaining ⅓ cup sauce mixture and turning every few minutes. Serve with reserved sauce mixture.   *Makes 4 servings*

Prep and cook time: 20 minutes

Nutrients per Serving:

Calories: 292, Total Fat: 5 g, Carbohydrate: 36 g, Sodium: 785 mg

Chicken in Wine Sauce

¼ cup all-purpose flour
1 teaspoon garlic-and-herb flavored no-salt
    seasoning mix
4 boneless, skinless chicken breasts, cut in
    ½-inch cubes
  Vegetable oil spray
2 cups sliced mushrooms
½ teaspoon minced garlic
1 (26-ounce) jar HEALTHY CHOICE®
    Traditional Pasta Sauce
¼ cup dry white wine
1 teaspoon dried basil
½ pound pasta noodles or shells, cooked and
    drained

In paper bag, combine flour and seasoning mix. Shake chicken in bag until lightly coated with flour mixture. Spray Dutch oven or large nonstick saucepan with pan coating; add chicken. Lightly brown chicken over medium heat. Add mushrooms and garlic; cook and stir until mushrooms are tender. Mix in pasta sauce, wine and basil. Simmer, covered, 10 minutes. Serve with pasta.   *Makes 6 servings*

Nutrients per Serving:

Calories: 357, Total Fat: 10 g, Cholesterol: 62 mg, Sodium: 445 mg

Tex-Mex Chicken Kabob

Chicken Marengo

1 tablespoon olive oil or vegetable oil
1 pound boneless skinless chicken breasts,
    cut into 1-inch pieces
3 small onions, each cut into 6 wedges
2 cloves garlic, minced
1 tablespoon all-purpose flour
1 cup chicken broth
¾ cup dry white wine
¼ cup tomato paste
4 ounces small mushrooms
2 (3×1-inch) strips orange peel
½ teaspoon dried thyme leaves
½ teaspoon dried tarragon leaves
3 cups cooked noodles or rice

1. Heat oil in large saucepan over medium-high heat until hot. Add chicken, onions and garlic; cook 5 minutes or until chicken is browned. Stir in flour; cook over medium heat 1 minute, stirring constantly.

2. Stir in chicken broth, wine, tomato paste, whole mushrooms, orange peel, thyme and tarragon; bring to a boil. Reduce heat to low; simmer, covered, 10 minutes or until chicken is tender. Season to taste with salt and pepper. Serve over noodles.   *Makes 4 (1-cup) servings*

Prep and cook time: 30 minutes

Nutrients per Serving:

Calories: 417, Total Fat: 9 g, Cholesterol: 113 mg, Sodium: 451 mg

Fantastic Feta Chicken

6 boneless skinless chicken breast halves
    (about 2 pounds)
2 tablespoons lemon juice, divided
2 teaspoons chopped fresh oregano *or*
    ¼ teaspoon dried oregano leaves
¼ teaspoon fresh ground pepper
1 package (4 ounces) ATHENOS®
    Crumbled Feta Cheese

ARRANGE chicken in 13×9-inch baking dish.

DRIZZLE with 1 tablespoon of the juice. Sprinkle with oregano and pepper; top with feta cheese and drizzle with remaining 1 tablespoon juice.

BAKE at 350°F for 30 to 35 minutes or until cooked through.   *Makes 6 servings*

Prep time: 35 minutes

Nutrients per Serving:

Calories: 220, Total Fat: 6 g, Cholesterol: 100 mg, Sodium: 220 mg

Chicken Marengo

Glazed Chicken, Carrots and Celery

1 cup uncooked rice
1 teaspoon dried dill weed
1 teaspoon dried parsley flakes
½ teaspoon salt
¼ teaspoon black pepper
1 pound chicken tenders
1 tablespoon vegetable oil
3 ribs celery, thinly sliced
2 carrots, thinly sliced
1 cup apple juice
1 chicken bouillon cube

1. Cook rice according to package directions, omitting salt.

2. While rice is cooking, mix dill, parsley, salt and pepper in medium bowl. Add chicken tenders.

3. Heat oil in nonstick skillet over medium heat. Add chicken, celery and carrots; cook and stir about 5 minutes or until chicken is tender.

4. Stir in apple juice and bouillon cube. Cook and stir over high heat about 10 minutes or until liquid has thickened and reduced to about 2 tablespoons. Serve over rice.   *Makes 4 servings*

Prep and cook time: 23 minutes

For a special touch, garnish with fresh sage leaves.

Nutrients per Serving:

Calories: 386, Total Fat: 7 g, Cholesterol: 69 mg, Sodium: 602 mg

Persian Chicken Breasts

Juice of 1 medium lemon
2 teaspoons olive oil
1 teaspoon ground cinnamon
½ teaspoon salt
¼ teaspoon ground black pepper
¼ teaspoon turmeric
4 boneless skinless chicken breast halves
4 flour tortillas or soft lavash

1. Combine juice with oil, cinnamon, salt, pepper and turmeric in large heavy-duty resealable plastic food storage bag; mix well. Add chicken; seal bag and turn to coat chicken. Refrigerate 4 hours or overnight.

2. Remove chicken from marinade and gently shake to remove excess. Grill chicken 5 to 7 minutes per side or until chicken is no longer pink in center, brushing occasionally with marinade. Discard remaining marinade. Serve chicken with lightly grilled tortillas or lavash.
Makes 4 servings

Nutrients per Servings:

Calories: 143, Total Fat: 4 g, Cholesterol: 69 mg, Sodium: 149 mg

Glazed Chicken, Carrots and Celery

Tangy Chicken Breasts with Citrus Sage Sauce

8 boneless skinless chicken breast halves (about 2 pounds)
6 ounces frozen lemonade concentrate, thawed
½ cup honey
1 teaspoon crushed dried sage leaves
½ teaspoon lemon juice
½ teaspoon crushed dried thyme leaves
½ teaspoon dry mustard

Rinse chicken breasts under cold water and pat dry with paper towels; place in shallow baking dish. Combine remaining ingredients in small bowl. Pour half the sauce over chicken and bake at 350°F 20 minutes. Turn chicken and pour remaining sauce over top. Bake 15 to 20 minutes more or until chicken is no longer pink in center.

Makes 8 servings

Nutrients per Serving:

Calories: 246, Total Fat: 3 g, Cholesterol: 69 mg, Sodium: 62 mg

Favorite recipe from **National Honey Board**

Zippy Orange Chicken and Rice

½ cup MIRACLE WHIP LIGHT® Salad Dressing, divided
4 boneless skinless chicken breast halves (about 1¼ pounds), cut into strips
½ cup orange juice
2 tablespoons brown sugar
1½ cups MINUTE® Original Rice, uncooked
1 green bell pepper, cut into strips
1 can (11 ounces) mandarin orange segments, drained *or* 1 orange, peeled, sectioned
1 can (8 ounces) pineapple chunks, drained

HEAT 2 tablespoons of the dressing in skillet on medium-high heat. Add chicken; cook and stir 5 minutes or until no longer pink. Drain. Reduce heat to medium.

MIX remaining dressing, juice and sugar. Stir into skillet. Add rice and bell pepper; bring to a boil.

REMOVE from heat; add orange segments and pineapple. Let stand, covered, 5 minutes.

Makes 4 servings

Prep time: 15 minutes

Nutrients per Serving:

Calories: 440, Total Fat: 8 g, Cholesterol: 90 mg, Sodium: 360 mg

Tangy Chicken Breast with Citrus Sage Sauce

Chicken Fajitas

2 tablespoons vegetable oil, divided
2 tablespoons fresh lime juice
2 teaspoons minced garlic
1 teaspoon dried oregano
½ teaspoon ground cumin
½ teaspoon red pepper flakes
¼ teaspoon salt
12 ounces boneless, skinless chicken breasts, pounded thin
4 flour tortillas (8-inch)
3 cups thin strips yellow onion, divided
12 tablespoons medium or hot salsa, divided
1 cup (4 ounces) shredded ALPINE LACE® Fat Free Pasteurized Process Skim Milk Cheese Product—For Cheddar Lovers, divided
1 cup chopped ripe tomatoes
1 small avocado, peeled, seeded and chopped (optional)
2 tablespoons minced fresh cilantro

1. In a large shallow glass dish, mix 1 tablespoon of the oil with the lime juice, garlic, oregano, cumin, red pepper flakes and salt. Add the chicken and turn to coat. Cover, refrigerate and marinate for 30 minutes.

2. Preheat the grill (or broiler and broiler pan). Wrap the tortillas in foil and place on the grill away from the direct heat (or in the oven). Pour the marinade from the chicken into a small saucepan; bring to boil.

3. Grill (or broil) the chicken, 4 inches from the heat, basting frequently with the hot marinade, for 6 to 8 minutes on each side or until the juices run clear when chicken is pierced with a fork. Transfer to a cutting board and slice into ¾-inch strips.

4. Meanwhile, in a medium-size nonstick skillet, sauté the onion in the remaining tablespoon of oil over medium-high heat for 8 minutes.

5. Unwrap the hot tortillas. For each fajita, spoon 2 tablespoons of salsa down the center of the tortilla. Top with a quarter of the chicken, onions and cheese. Roll up and place, seam side down, on a warm platter. Top each fajita with 1 tablespoon of the remaining salsa, some of the chopped tomatoes, avocado, if you wish, and the cilantro.   *Makes 4 fajitas*

Nutrients per Serving:

Calories: 382, Total Fat: 11 g, Cholesterol: 54 mg

Roasted Rosemary-Lemon Chicken

1 whole chicken (3¼ pounds)
½ teaspoon ground black pepper
1 lemon, cut into eighths
¼ cup fresh parsley
4 sprigs fresh rosemary
3 fresh sage leaves
2 sprigs fresh thyme
1 can (about 14 ounces) fat-free reduced-
  sodium chicken broth
1 cup sliced onions
4 cloves garlic
1 cup thinly sliced carrots
1 cup thinly sliced zucchini

1. Preheat oven to 350°F. Trim fat from chicken, leaving skin on. Rinse chicken and pat dry with paper towels. Fill cavity of chicken with black pepper, lemon, parsley, rosemary, sage and thyme. Close cavity with skewers.

2. Combine broth, onions and garlic in heavy roasting pan. Place chicken on rack over broth. Bake 1½ hours or until juices run clear when pierced with fork. Remove chicken to serving plate.

3. Combine carrots and zucchini in small saucepan with tight-fitting lid. Cover and steam 4 minutes or until vegetables are crisp-tender. Transfer vegetables to colander; drain.

4. Remove skewers. Discard lemon and herbs from cavity of chicken. Remove skin from chicken. Cut chicken into pieces. Remove onions and garlic from pan with slotted spoon to medium serving bowl or plate. Add carrots and zucchini; mix well. Arrange vegetable mixture around chicken. Garnish with fresh rosemary sprigs and lemon slices, if desired.   *Makes 6 servings*

Note: Cooking chicken with skin on insulates the chicken, keeping it tender and moist. Removing the skin just before serving reduces fat almost as much as cooking chicken without the skin.

Nutrients per Serving:

Calories: 282, Total Fat: 10 g, Cholesterol: 120 mg, Sodium: 133 mg

Chicken Cacciatore

4 pounds chicken pieces with bone (breasts, legs, thighs)
¾ teaspoon salt
¾ teaspoon freshly ground black pepper
⅓ cup all-purpose flour
1 tablespoon fresh oregano leaves or
    1 teaspoon dried oregano
3 tablespoons olive oil, divided
2 teaspoons minced garlic
1 cup chopped yellow onion
3 cups (8 ounces) sliced mushrooms
2 cups red bell pepper strips
3 cups fresh ripe tomato wedges
⅔ cup red wine (with or without alcohol)
⅓ cup low-salt tomato juice
1 tablespoon fresh rosemary leaves or
    1 teaspoon dried rosemary
2 cups (8 ounces) shredded ALPINE
    LACE® Fat Free Pasteurized Process
    Skim Milk Cheese Product—For
    Mozzarella Lovers
¼ cup minced fresh parsley

1. Rinse the chicken and pat dry with paper towels. Sprinkle with the salt and black pepper. In a large self-sealing plastic bag, combine the flour and oregano. Add the chicken and shake well.

2. In a large deep nonstick skillet, heat 2 tablespoons of the oil over medium-high heat. Add the chicken pieces in batches and cook, turning occasionally, for 8 minutes or until golden brown. Transfer to a plate.

3. Add the remaining tablespoon of oil to the skillet with the garlic and onion. Sauté for 5 minutes or until soft. Add the mushrooms and bell peppers and sauté 5 minutes longer. Stir in the tomatoes, wine, tomato juice and rosemary. Return the chicken to the skillet and bring to a boil. Reduce the heat. Cover; simmer, turning the chicken occasionally, for 30 minutes or until juices run clear.

4. Preheat the broiler. Sprinkle the chicken with the cheese and broil for 3 minutes or just until melted. Garnish with the parsley.

Makes 6 servings

Nutrients per Serving:

Calories: 310, Total Fat: 10 g, Cholesterol: 62 mg

Stuffed Chicken Breasts à la Française

6 boneless, skinless chicken breast halves, with pockets (6 ounces each)
6 ounces (1 carton) ALPINE LACE® Fat Free Cream Cheese with Garlic & Herbs
½ cup finely chopped green onions (tops only)
2 teaspoons snipped fresh rosemary leaves or ¾ teaspoon dried rosemary
½ cup all-purpose flour
1 teaspoon freshly ground black pepper
⅓ cup low sodium chicken broth
⅓ cup dry white wine or low sodium chicken broth
8 sprigs fresh rosemary, about 3 inches long (optional)

1. Preheat the oven to 350°F. Spray a 13×9×2-inch baking dish with nonstick cooking spray. Rinse the chicken and pat dry with paper towels. In a medium-size bowl, mix the cream cheese with the green onions and rosemary until well blended. Stuff the pockets of the chicken breasts with the mixture.

2. On a piece of wax paper, blend the flour and pepper. Roll each chicken breast in the seasoned flour, then arrange in the baking dish. Pour over the broth and the wine.

3. Cover the dish tightly with foil and bake for 30 minutes. Uncover and bake 10 minutes more or until the juices run clear when the thickest piece of chicken is pierced with a fork.

4. Transfer the chicken to a serving platter and garnish each with a sprig of rosemary, if you wish.
Makes 6 servings

Nutrients per Serving:

Calories: 274, Total Fat: 3 g, Cholesterol: 107 mg

Spicy Mesquite Chicken Fettuccine

8 ounces uncooked fettuccine
1 tablespoon chili powder
1 teaspoon ground cumin
1 teaspoon paprika
¼ teaspoon ground red pepper
2 teaspoons vegetable oil
1 pound mesquite marinated chicken breasts, cut into bite-size pieces

1. Cook pasta according to package directions, omitting salt. Drain; set aside.

2. Combine chili powder, cumin, paprika and ground red pepper in small bowl; set aside.

3. Heat oil in large nonstick skillet over medium-high heat until hot. Add chili powder mixture; cook 30 seconds, stirring constantly. Add chicken; cook and stir 5 to 6 minutes or until no longer pink in center and lightly browned. Add pasta to skillet; stir. Cook 1 to 2 minutes or until heated through. Sprinkle with additional chili powder, if desired.
Makes 4 servings

Nutrients per Serving:

Calories: 520, Total Fat: 8 g, Cholesterol: 144 mg, Sodium: 699 mg

Corny Chicken Pot Pie

CHICKEN FILLING

   1 tablespoon unsalted butter substitute
   3 tablespoons all-purpose flour
   ¾ cup low-sodium chicken broth
   ½ cup 2% low fat milk
   6 ounces (1 carton) ALPINE LACE® Fat
      Free Cream Cheese with Garden
      Vegetables
   ¼ teaspoon salt, or to taste
   ¼ teaspoon freshly ground black pepper
   2 cups (12 ounces) small chunks cooked
      skinless chicken breast
   1 package (10 ounces) frozen mixed
      vegetables, thawed and drained
   1 cup (6 ounces) small chunks ALPINE
      LACE® 97% Fat Free Boneless Cooked
      Ham

CORN BREAD CRUST

   1 package (8½ ounces) corn bread mix
   ¼ cup egg substitute or 1 large egg
   ⅓ cup 2% low fat milk

1. Preheat the oven to 425°F. Spray six (6-inch) individual au gratin dishes or six (2-cup) baking dishes with nonstick cooking spray. Set aside.

2. To make the Chicken Filling: In a medium-size saucepan, melt butter over medium heat. Whisk in flour; cook 3 minutes, stirring constantly. Gradually whisk in the chicken broth, the ½ cup milk, the cream cheese, salt and pepper. Cook, whisking occasionally, for 5 minutes or until thickened. Stir in the chicken, vegetables and ham. Cook for 2 minutes or until hot. Divide the filling evenly among the 6 dishes.

3. To make the Corn Bread Crust: In a medium-size bowl, whisk the corn bread mix, the egg substitute (or the whole egg) and the ⅓ cup of milk. (Batter will be slightly lumpy.) Drop heaping tablespoons of batter (about ¼ cup) on top of each of the 6 pies, dividing the batter evenly. Bake, uncovered, for 15 minutes or until the corn bread is golden brown.

Makes 6 servings

Nutrients per Serving:

Calories: 369, Total Fat: 9 g, Cholesterol: 55 mg

Easy Chicken Fettuccine

   8 ounces plain or spinach fettuccine
   2 skinless boneless chicken breast halves
      (about ¾ pound), cut into chunks
   ½ cup skim milk
   ¼ cup soft reduced-calorie margarine
   ¾ cup (3 ounces) KRAFT® FREE® Nonfat
      Grated Topping
   ¾ teaspoon garlic powder
   ¼ teaspoon pepper

COOK fettuccine as directed on package; drain. Meanwhile, cook chicken in skillet sprayed with nonstick cooking spray until cooked through.

ADD milk and margarine to hot fettuccine.

STIR in chicken, grated topping and seasonings.

Makes 6 servings

Nutrients per Serving:

Calories: 300, Total Fat: 6 g, Cholesterol: 40 mg, Sodium: 340 mg

Corny Chicken Pot Pie

Glazed Chicken & Vegetable Skewers

GOLDEN GLAZE

¼ cup apricot or peach preserves
2 tablespoons spicy brown mustard
2 cloves garlic, minced

CHICKEN & VEGETABLE SKEWERS

12 small red or new potatoes
1 pound boneless skinless chicken thighs or breasts, cut into 1-inch pieces
1 yellow or red bell pepper, cut into 1-inch pieces
½ small red onion, cut into 1-inch pieces

1. For glaze, combine preserves, mustard and garlic in small bowl; mix well. Set aside. Prepare barbecue grill for direct cooking.

2. Place potatoes in large saucepan; cover with water. Bring to a boil over high heat. Cook 10 minutes or until almost tender. Rinse with cool water; drain.

3. Alternately thread chicken, potatoes, bell pepper and onion onto skewers. Brush glaze evenly over both sides.

4. Place skewers on grid over medium-hot coals. Grill, on covered grill, 14 minutes for chicken breast or 16 minutes for chicken thighs or until chicken is no longer pink in center and vegetables are crisp-tender, turning once.

Makes 4 servings

Nutrients per Serving:

Calories: 272, Total Fat: 6 g, Cholesterol: 46 mg, Sodium: 153 mg

Grilled Chicken Dijon Salad

¼ cup Dijon mustard
2 teaspoons crushed dried tarragon leaves
¼ teaspoon cracked black pepper
3 tablespoons tarragon vinegar
⅓ cup water
1 tablespoon sugar
2 tablespoons plus 2 teaspoons olive oil
2 whole chicken breasts, skinned, boned, fat removed
½ pound mushrooms, cleaned, cut in half
2 cups broccoli florets
5 cups torn Boston lettuce
5 cups torn red leaf lettuce
1 (8-ounce) package HEALTHY CHOICE® Fat Free Natural Fancy Shredded Mozzarella Cheese
½ cup red onion rings

Mix together mustard, tarragon and pepper; stir in vinegar, water and sugar. Gradually add oil, beating until well blended. Pour ⅓ cup of dressing mixture over chicken. Marinate mushrooms and broccoli in remaining dressing.

Drain chicken, reserving marinade. Grill chicken over medium coals, 4 minutes on each side or until no longer pink in center, brushing with reserved marinade mixture before turning. Cut chicken into 8 strips.

Toss mushrooms, broccoli and marinade with lettuce and cheese in serving bowl. Arrange lettuce mixture on large platter; top with chicken and onion rings. *Makes 8 servings*

Nutrients per Serving:

Calories: 170, Total Fat: 6 g, Cholesterol: 30 mg, Sodium: 343 mg

Glazed Chicken & Vegetable Skewers

Sesame Chicken and Vegetable Stir-Fry

1 tablespoon dark sesame oil
1 pound chicken tenders, cut into 1-inch
    pieces
2 cups broccoli florets
1 small red bell pepper, sliced
½ cup onion slices (about 1 small)
½ cup snow peas
1 can (8 ounces) water chestnuts, sliced and
    drained
2 cloves garlic, minced
1 teaspoon Chinese five-spice powder
1 cup fat-free reduced-sodium chicken broth
2 teaspoons cornstarch
2 tablespoons cold water
2 cups hot cooked rice

1. Heat sesame oil in wok or large nonstick skillet over medium heat until hot. Add chicken; stir-fry about 8 minutes or until chicken is no longer pink in center. Remove chicken from wok.

2. Add broccoli, bell pepper, onion, peas, water chestnuts and garlic to wok; stir-fry 5 to 8 minutes or until vegetables are crisp-tender. Sprinkle with five-spice powder; cook and stir 1 minute.

3. Return chicken to wok. Add chicken broth; heat to a boil. Combine cornstarch and water in small bowl; stir into broth mixture. Boil 1 to 2 minutes, stirring constantly. Serve over rice.

Makes 4 servings

Nutrients per Serving:

Calories: 354, Total Fat: 7 g, Cholesterol: 59 mg, Sodium: 83 mg

Curried Chicken Cutlets

4 boneless skinless chicken breast halves
½ cup all-purpose flour
1 tablespoon curry powder
1 teaspoon salt
1 teaspoon ground red pepper
2 red bell peppers, cut lengthwise into
    ¼-inch-thick slices
1 teaspoon olive oil
¼ cup lemon juice
¼ cup finely chopped fresh cilantro

1. Pound chicken breasts to ¼-inch thickness between 2 pieces of plastic wrap with flat side of meat mallet or rolling pin.

2. Combine flour, curry powder, salt and ground red pepper in shallow bowl. Dip chicken in flour mixture to coat both sides well; shake off excess flour.

3. Generously spray nonstick skillet with nonstick cooking spray; heat over medium heat. Add 2 chicken cutlets; cook 3 to 4 minutes per side. Transfer to warm plate; cover and set aside. Repeat with remaining chicken.

4. Add bell peppers and olive oil to skillet; cook and stir 5 minutes or until peppers are tender. Stir in lemon juice and cilantro; heat through. Pour sauce over chicken cutlets.

Makes 4 servings

Nutrients per Serving:

Calories: 230, Total Fat: 5 g, Cholesterol: 73 mg, Sodium: 599 mg

ACKNOWLEDGMENTS

The publisher would like to thank the companies and organizations listed below for the use of their recipes and photographs in this publication.

Alpine Lace Brands, Inc.

American Italian Pasta Company

Birds Eye®

Blue Diamond Growers®

Chef Paul Prudhomme's Magic Seasoning Blends®

Cherry Marketing Institute, Inc.

COLLEGE INN® Broth

Delmarva Poultry Industry, Inc.

Del Monte Corporation

Diamond Walnut Growers, Inc.

Farmhouse Foods Company

Filippo Berio Olive Oil

GREY POUPON® Mustard

Guiltless Gourmet, Incorporated

Healthy Choice®

Kikkoman International Inc.

The Kingsford Products Company

Kraft Foods, Inc.

Lawry's® Foods, Inc.

Lipton™

McCormick®/Schilling®

McIlhenny Company

National Broiler Council

National Honey Board

Nestlé USA

Perdue Farms Incorporated

PLANTERS® Peanuts

Reckitt & Colman Inc.

Riviana Foods Inc.

Sargento® Foods Inc.

Sonoma® Dried Tomatoes

The Sugar Association, Inc.

USA Rice Federation

Wesson/Peter Pan Foods Company

Wisconsin Milk Marketing Board

INDEX

A

Alfalfa Sprouts: San Francisco Grilled
    Chicken Sandwiches, 28
All-American Barbecued Roaster, 146
Almonds
    Almond-Crusted Chicken Breasts, 114
    Chicken Breasts with Orange-Lime Sauce,
    124
    Indian-Spiced Chicken with Wild Rice,
    62
    Mandarin Chicken Salad, 14
    One-Pot Chicken Couscous, 76
Apples
    Apple-Stuffed Chicken, 122
    Chicken Curry, 80
    Country Chicken Stew, 96
    Stuffed Chicken with Apple Glaze, 100
Apricot Glazed Chicken, 154
Arroz con Pollo, 92
Artichoke Hearts: Artichoke-Olive
    Chicken Bake, 54
Asparagus
    Chicken and Asparagus Hollandaise, 148
    Chicken and Asparagus Stir-Fry, 136
    Chicken-Asparagus Casserole, 60
Avocados
    Chicken Fajitas, 172
    Chicken Santa Fe, 126
    Open-Faced Chicken Sandwiches with
    Broiled Vegetables, 18
    San Francisco Grilled Chicken
    Sandwiches, 28

B

Bacon
    Chicken Santa Fe, 126
    Country Chicken Stew, 96
    Southern-Style Chicken and Greens, 88
Baked Barbecue Chicken, 129
Bamboo Shoots: Hot and Sour Soup, 16

Barbecue Sauce
    Barbecue Chicken with Cornbread
    Topper, 56
    Barbecued Chicken Pizza, 162
    Barbecued Orange Chicken, 148
    Tex-Mex Chicken Kabobs, 164
Barley: Chicken-Barley Soup, 24
Basil
    Basil, Chicken and Vegetables on
    Focaccia, 12
    Chicken with Orange and Basil, 112
    Lemon Basil Chicken, 150
    Thai Chicken with Basil, 48
Beans
    Barbecue Chicken with Cornbread
    Topper, 56
    Chicken and Black Bean Enchiladas, 68
    Chicken Pot Pie, 70
    Country Chicken Stew, 96
    Mexicali Chicken Stew, 94
    Mexican Chicken Stew, 80
    Mexican Chicken Stir-Fry, 44
    Southwest White Chili, 22
Bean Sprouts
    Easy Oriental Chicken Sandwiches, 20
    Mandarin Chicken Salad, 14
    Thai Chicken Sandwiches, 16
Broccoli
    Chicken & Pasta Toss with Sun-Dried
    Tomatoes, 84
    Chicken and Vegetable Chowder, 26
    Chicken Cacciatore, 152
    Chicken Primavera, 114
    Chicken Salad Primavera in Pita, 20
    Chicken Stir-Fry, 40
    First Moon Chicken Stir-Fry, 44
    Grilled Chicken Dijon Salad, 180
    Grilled Chicken Pasta Toss, 104
    Lemon Pepper Pasta with Chicken and
    Dijon Teriyaki Sauce, 90
    Rotelle with Grilled Chicken Dijon, 76
    Sesame Chicken and Vegetable Stir-Fry,
    182

Broccoli *(continued)*
    Snappy Chicken and Vegetables, 94
    Spicy Chicken Stromboli, 134
    Szechuan Stir-Fry, 50
    Warm Chicken and Rice Salad, 26
Broiled Chicken with Honeyed Onion
    Sauce, 102
Buffalo Chicken Drumsticks, 116
Buttermilk Ranch Fried Chicken, 132

C

Cabbage
    Chicken & Cabbage Stir-Fry, 38
    Mandarin Chicken Salad, 24
    Oriental Chicken Cabbage, 18
    Reuben Chicken Melts, 154
Caesar Chicken Salad, 158
Caesar Chicken Sandwiches, 22
Cajun Chicken Burgers, 129
Carrots
    Chicken & Cabbage Stir-Fry, 38
    Chicken & Vegetable Chowder, 26
    Chicken-Barley Soup, 24
    Chicken Cacciatore, 152
    Chicken Pot Pie, 70
    Chicken Salad Primavera in Pita, 20
    Chicken Stir-Fry, 40
    Country Chicken Stew, 96
    First Moon Chicken Stir-Fry, 44
    Gazebo Chicken, 14
    Glazed Chicken, Carrots and Celery, 168
    Grilled Chicken Pasta Toss, 104
    Honey Nut Stir-Fry, 42
    Hot and Sour Soup, 16
    Indian-Spiced Chicken with Wild Rice,
    62
    Lemon Cashew Chicken Stir-Fry, 46
    Lemon Chicken with Walnuts, 82
    Mandarin Chicken Salad, 14
    One-Pot Chicken Couscous, 76
    Oriental Chicken Cabbage, 18

186

Carrots (*continued*)
Roasted Rosemary-Lemon Chicken, 173
Savory Chicken & Biscuits, 68
Spicy Chicken Salad in Peanut Sauce, 28
Sweet & Sour Cashew Chicken, 42
Thai Chicken Sandwiches, 16

Cashews
Honey Nut Stir-Fry, 42
Lemon Cashew Chicken Stir-Fry, 46
Sweet & Sour Cashew Chicken, 42

Cheese (*see also* **Cream Cheese**)
Artichoke-Olive Chicken Bake, 54
Barbecued Chicken Pizza, 162
Buffalo Chicken Drumsticks, 116
Caesar Chicken Salad, 158
Chicken and Black Bean Enchiladas, 68
Chicken & Pasta Toss with Sun-Dried
Tomatoes, 84
Chicken-Asparagus Casserole, 60
Chicken Breasts Smothered in Tomatoes
and Mozzarella, 156
Chicken Cacciatore, 174
Chicken Cordon Bleu, 118
Chicken Cordon Bleu Bake, 58
Chicken Fajitas, 172
Chicken Parmesan Noodle Bake, 140
Chicken Pesto Mozzarella, 108
Chicken-Pesto Pizza, 144
Chicken Santa Fe, 126
Chicken Tetrazzini, 54, 66
Chicken Tetrazzini with Roasted Red
Peppers, 84
Chile Rellenos-Style Chicken, 138
Chili Pepper Pasta Santa Fe Style, 86
Easy Chicken Fettuccine, 178
Fantastic Feta Chicken, 166
Grilled Chicken Dijon Salad, 180
Mustard-Glazed Chicken Sandwiches, 142
Ortega® Chicken Fajitas, 90
Reuben Chicken Melts, 154
Roasted Chicken and Vegetables over
Wild Rice, 52
San Francisco Grilled Chicken
Sandwiches, 28
Spicy Chicken Stromboli, 134
Spicy Chicken Tortilla Casserole, 56
Thai Chicken Sandwiches, 16
Cherry-Glazed Chicken, 130

Chicken, Cooked
Artichoke-Olive Chicken Bake, 54
Chicken and Black Bean Enchiladas, 68

Chicken, Cooked (*continued*)
Chicken-Asparagus Casserole, 60
Chicken-Barley Soup, 24
Chicken Cordon Bleu Bake, 58
Chicken Salad Primavera in Pita, 20
Chicken Tetrazzini, 54, 66
Chicken Tetrazzini with Roasted Red
Peppers, 84
Corny Chicken Pot Pie, 178
Jiffy Chicken Supper, 88
Oriental Chicken Cabbage, 18
Southwestern Chicken Soup, 23
Southwest Skillet, 78
Spicy Chicken Salad in Peanut Sauce, 28
Spicy Chicken Stromboli, 134

Chicken, Cut Up
Apricot Glazed Chicken, 154
Baked Barbecue Chicken, 129
Buttermilk Ranch Fried Chicken, 132
Cherry-Glazed Chicken, 130
Chicken and Andouille Gumbo, 23
Chicken Cacciatore, 174
Chicken Fiesta, 72
Coq au Vin, 74
Country Herb Roasted Chicken, 138
Creole Chicken, 86
Crispy Ranch Chicken, 144
Drunken Chicken, 82
Lemon Basil Chicken, 150
Little Italy Chicken and Rice, 60
Marinated Mustard Chicken, 102
Oven Chicken & Rice, 72
Roasted Chicken and Vegetables over
Wild Rice, 52
Santa Fe Grilled Chicken, 104
Southern Fried Chicken, 110
Southern-Style Chicken and Greens, 88

Chicken, Deli: Peppy Pesto Toss, 152
Chicken, Ground: Cajun Chicken Burgers,
129

Chicken, Whole
All-American Barbecued Roaster, 146
Apple-Stuffed Chicken, 122
Chinese Roaster, 146
French Roaster, 146
German Roaster, 146
Italian Roaster, 146
Roast Chicken Florentine, 106
Roast Chicken Spanish Style, 112
Roasted Rosemary-Lemon Chicken, 173
Stuffed Chicken with Apple Glaze, 100

Chicken and Andouille Gumbo, 23
Chicken and Asparagus Hollandaise, 148
Chicken and Asparagus Stir-Fry, 136
Chicken and Black Bean Enchiladas, 68
Chicken & Cabbage Stir-Fry, 38
Chicken & Pasta Toss with Sun-Dried
Tomatoes, 84
Chicken & Rice Bake, 70
Chicken and Vegetable Chowder, 26
Chicken and Vegetables with Mustard
Sauce, 36
Chicken-Asparagus Casserole, 60
Chicken-Barley Soup, 24

Chicken Breasts, Bone-In
Chicken & Rice Bake, 70
Crispy Baked Chicken, 160
Mandarin Chicken Salad, 14
Quick-as-a-Wink Chicken, 156

Chicken Breasts, Boneless
Almond-Crusted Chicken Breasts, 114
Arroz con Pollo, 92
Barbecue Chicken with Cornbread
Topper, 56
Barbecued Chicken Pizza, 162
Basil, Chicken and Vegetables on
Focaccia, 12
Caesar Chicken Salad, 158
Caesar Chicken Sandwiches, 22
Chicken and Asparagus Hollandaise, 148
Chicken and Asparagus Stir-Fry, 136
Chicken & Cabbage Stir-Fry, 38
Chicken & Pasta Toss with Sun-Dried
Tomatoes, 84
Chicken and Vegetable Chowder, 26
Chicken and Vegetables with Mustard
Sauce, 36
Chicken Breasts Smothered in Tomatoes
and Mozzarella, 156
Chicken Breasts with Orange-Lime Sauce,
124
Chicken Cacciatore, 152
Chicken Cordon Bleu, 118
Chicken Curry, 80
Chicken Fajitas, 172
Chicken Fried Rice, 36
Chicken in Cream Sauce, 96
Chicken in Wine Sauce, 164
Chicken Marengo, 166
Chicken Marsala, 78
Chicken Parmesan, 64
Chicken Parmesan Noodle Bake, 140

Chicken Breasts, Boneless (*continued*)
Chicken Pasta, 92
Chicken Pesto Mozzarella, 108
Chicken Pesto Tortelloni, 132
Chicken Primavera, 114
Chicken Santa Fe, 126
Chicken Stir-Fry, 40
Chicken with Orange and Basil, 112
Chicken with Walnuts, 34
Chile Rellenos-Style Chicken, 138
Chili Pepper Pasta Santa Fe Style, 86
Cilantro-Lime Chicken, 50
Country Chicken in Rich Onion Gravy, 128
Country Chicken Stew, 96
Creamy Herbed Chicken, 38
Curried Chicken Cutlets, 182
Dijon-Chicken Spirals, 110
Easy Chicken Fettuccine, 178
Easy Oriental Chicken Sandwiches, 20
Fantastic Feta Chicken, 166
First Moon Chicken Stir-Fry, 44
Gazebo Chicken, 14
Grilled Chicken Dijon Salad, 180
Grilled Chicken Pasta Toss, 104
Grilled Chicken with Orange-Cilantro Salsa, 126
Grilled Ginger Chicken with Pineapple and Coconut Rice, 160
Grilled Rosemary Chicken, 106
Hoisin Chicken Breasts Supreme, 116
Honey-Mustard Glazed Chicken, 140
Honey Nut Stir-Fry, 42
Hot and Sour Soup, 16
Indian-Spiced Chicken with Wild Rice, 62
Jamaican Rum Chicken, 120
Kung Pao Chicken, 40
Lemon Chicken with Walnuts, 82
Lemon-Herb Chicken, 147
Lemon Pepper Pasta with Chicken and Dijon Teriyaki Sauce, 90
Mandarin Chicken Salad, 24
Mediterranean Chicken Salad Sandwiches, 32
Mexican Chicken Stew, 80
Minute® Easy Chicken Stir-Fry, 147
Mustard-Glazed Chicken Sandwiches, 142
One-Dish Chicken 'n' Rice, 62
One-Dish Chicken Bake, 158

Chicken Breasts, Boneless (*continued*)
One-Pot Chicken Couscous, 76
Open-Faced Chicken Sandwiches with Broiled Vegetables, 18
Ortega® Chicken Fajitas, 90
Persian Chicken Breasts, 168
Pollo Verde Casserole, 64
Reuben Chicken Melts, 154
Rotelle with Grilled Chicken Dijon, 76
San Francisco Grilled Chicken Sandwiches, 28
Savory Chicken & Biscuits, 68
Simple Marinated Chicken Breasts, 108
Snappy Chicken and Vegetables, 94
Southwestern Style Stir-Fry, 46
Southwest White Chili, 22
Spanish Skillet Supper, 142
Spicy Chicken Tortilla Casserole, 56
Spicy Mesquite Chicken Fettuccine, 176
Stuffed Chicken Breasts à la Française, 176
Summer Caesar Salad, 30
Sweet & Sour Cashew Chicken, 42
Sweet and Sour Chicken, 48
Tangy Chicken Breasts with Citrus Sage Sauce, 170
Thai Chicken Sandwiches, 16
Thai Chicken with Basil, 48
Warm Chicken and Rice Salad, 26
Warm Chicken Taco Salad, 32
Zippy Orange Chicken and Rice, 170
Chicken Breasts Smothered in Tomatoes and Mozzarella, 156
Chicken Cacciatore, 152, 174
Chicken Cordon Bleu, 118
Chicken Cordon Bleu Bake, 58
Chicken Curry, 80
Chicken Drumsticks
Buffalo Chicken Drumsticks, 116
Cornmeal-Crusted Drums, 120
Chicken Fajitas, 172
Chicken Fiesta, 72
Chicken Fried Rice, 36
Chicken in Cream Sauce, 96
Chicken in Wine Sauce, 164
Chicken Legs: Grilled Marinated Chicken, 130
Chicken Marengo, 166
Chicken Marsala, 78
Chicken Parmesan, 64
Chicken Parmesan Noodle Bake, 140

Chicken Pasta, 92
Chicken Pesto Mozzarella, 108
Chicken-Pesto Pizza, 144
Chicken Pesto Tortelloni, 132
Chicken Pot Pie, 70
Chicken Primavera, 114
Chicken Provençale, 98
Chicken Quarters
Barbecued Orange Chicken, 148
Honey-Lime Glazed Chicken, 150
Honey Roasted Chicken, 147
Lemon Pepper Chicken, 134
Chicken Salad Primavera in Pita, 20
Chicken Santa Fe, 126
Chicken Stir-Fry, 40
Chicken Tenders
Chicken-Pesto Pizza, 144
Country Chicken Chowder, 30
Glazed Chicken, Carrots and Celery, 168
Lemon Cashew Chicken Stir-Fry, 46
Mexican Chicken Stir-Fry, 44
Sesame Chicken and Vegetable Stir-Fry, 182
Tex-Mex Chicken Kabobs, 164
Chicken Tetrazzini, 54, 66
Chicken Tetrazzini with Roasted Red Peppers, 84
Chicken Thighs
Barbecue Chicken with Cornbread Topper, 56
Broiled Chicken with Honeyed Onion Sauce, 102
Chicken Fried Rice, 36
Chicken Pot Pie, 70
Chicken Provençale, 98
Chicken Salad Primavera in Pita, 20
Chicky Quicky, 150
Country Chicken Stew, 96
Creole Chicken Thighs & Rice, 98
Gingered Chicken Thighs, 124
Glazed Chicken & Vegetable Skewers, 180
Grilled Chicken with Pesto Sauce, 118
Kung Pao Chicken, 40
Mexicali Chicken Stew, 94
Quick Chicken Pot Pie, 58
Chicken Wings
Hot & Spicy Arroz con Pollo, 66
Szechuan Stir-Fry, 50
Chicken with Orange and Basil, 112
Chicken with Walnuts, 34

Chicky Quicky, 150
Chile Rellenos-Style Chicken, 138
Chili Pepper Pasta Santa Fe Style, 86
Chinese Roaster, 146
Cilantro
   Chili Pepper Pasta Santa Fe Style, 86
   Cilantro-Lime Chicken, 50
   Grilled Chicken with Orange-Cilantro
      Salsa, 126
Coconut: Grilled Ginger Chicken with
      Pineapple and Coconut Rice, 160
Coq au Vin, 74
Corn
   Chicken and Vegetable Chowder, 26
   Chicken Fiesta, 72
   Country Chicken Chowder, 30
   Mexicali Chicken Stew, 94
   Mexican Chicken Stew, 80
   Southwestern Chicken Soup, 23
   Thai Chicken with Basil, 48
Corn Bread Mix
   Barbecue Chicken with Cornbread
      Topper, 56
   Corny Chicken Pot Pie, 178
Cornflake Crumbs
   Crispy Baked Chicken, 160
   Crispy Ranch Chicken, 144
Cornmeal-Crusted Drums, 120
Corny Chicken Pot Pie, 178
Country Chicken Chowder, 30
Country Chicken in Rich Onion Gravy,
   128
Country Chicken Stew, 96
Country Herb Roasted Chicken, 138
Couscous: One-Pot Chicken Couscous, 76
Cream Cheese
   Apple-Stuffed Chicken, 122
   Chicken in Cream Sauce, 96
   Corny Chicken Pot Pie, 178
   Creamy Herbed Chicken, 38
   Stuffed Chicken Breasts à la Française,
      176
Creole Chicken, 86
Creole Chicken Thighs & Rice, 98
Crispy Baked Chicken, 160
Crispy Ranch Chicken, 144
Cucumbers
   Easy Oriental Chicken Sandwiches, 20
   Mediterranean Chicken Salad
      Sandwiches, 32
Curried Chicken Cutlets, 182

D

Dijon-Chicken Spirals, 110
Drunken Chicken, 82

E

Easy Chicken Fettuccine, 178
Easy Oriental Chicken Sandwiches, 20
Eggplants
   Chicken Provençale, 98
   Roasted Chicken and Vegetables over
      Wild Rice, 52

F

Fantastic Feta Chicken, 166
First Moon Chicken Stir-Fry, 44
French Roaster, 146

G

Gazebo Chicken, 14
German Roaster, 146
Gingered Chicken Thighs, 124
Glazed Chicken, Carrots and Celery, 168
Glazed Chicken & Vegetable Skewers, 180
Green Onions
   Chicken and Andouille Gumbo, 23
   Chicken Fiesta, 72
   Chicken Fried Rice, 36
   Chicken Pasta, 92
   Mandarin Chicken Salad, 14
   Oriental Chicken Cabbage, 18
   Sweet and Sour Chicken, 48
   Thai Chicken Sandwiches, 16
Greens: Southern-Style Chicken and
      Greens, 88
Grilled Chicken Dijon Salad, 180
Grilled Chicken Pasta Toss, 104
Grilled Chicken with Orange-Cilantro
      Salsa, 126
Grilled Chicken with Pesto Sauce, 118
Grilled Ginger Chicken with Pineapple and
      Coconut Rice, 160
Grilled Marinated Chicken, 130
Grilled Rosemary Chicken, 106
Guacamole: Ortega® Chicken Fajitas, 90

H

Ham
   Chicken Cordon Bleu, 118
   Chicken Cordon Bleu Bake, 58
   Corny Chicken Pot Pie, 178
Hoisin Chicken Breasts Supreme, 116
Honey
   Broiled Chicken with Honeyed Onion
      Sauce, 102
   Honey-Lime Glazed Chicken, 150
   Honey-Mustard Glazed Chicken, 140
   Honey Nut Stir-Fry, 42
   Honey Roasted Chicken, 147
   Tangy Chicken Breasts with Citrus Sage
      Sauce, 170
Hot and Sour Soup, 16
Hot & Spicy Arroz con Pollo, 66

I

Indian-Spiced Chicken with Wild Rice, 62
Italian Roaster, 146

J

Jamaican Rum Chicken, 120
Jicama: Chili Pepper Pasta Santa Fe Style,
   86
Jiffy Chicken Supper, 88

K

Ketchup: Baked Barbecue Chicken, 129
Kung Pao Chicken, 40

L

Leeks
   Chili Pepper Pasta Santa Fe Style, 86
   Country Chicken Stew, 96
Lemon
   Grilled Marinated Chicken, 130
   Lemon Basil Chicken, 150
   Lemon Cashew Chicken Stir-Fry, 46
   Lemon Chicken with Walnuts, 82
   Lemon-Herb Chicken, 147

Lemon (*continued*)
Lemon Pepper Chicken, 134
Roasted Rosemary-Lemon Chicken, 173
Tangy Chicken Breasts with Citrus Sage Sauce, 170
Lime
Chicken Breasts with Orange-Lime Sauce, 124
Cilantro-Lime Chicken, 50
Honey-Lime Glazed Chicken, 150
Little Italy Chicken and Rice, 60

M

Mandarin Chicken Salad, 14, 24
Marinated Mustard Chicken, 102
Mediterranean Chicken Salad Sandwiches, 32
Mexicali Chicken Stew, 94
Mexican Chicken Stew, 80
Mexican Chicken Stir-Fry, 44
Minute® Easy Chicken Stir-Fry, 147
Mushrooms
Barbecued Chicken Pizza, 162
Chicken & Rice Bake, 70
Chicken and Vegetable Chowder, 26
Chicken Cacciatore, 174
Chicken Fried Rice, 36
Chicken in Wine Sauce, 164
Chicken Marengo, 166
Chicken Marsala, 78
Chicken Pasta, 92
Chicken Tetrazzini, 54
Chicken Tetrazzini with Roasted Red Peppers, 84
Coq au Vin, 74
Drunken Chicken, 82
Grilled Chicken Dijon Salad, 180
Hot and Sour Soup, 16
Lemon Cashew Chicken Stir-Fry, 46
Lemon Pepper Pasta with Chicken and Dijon Teriyaki Sauce, 90
Open-Faced Chicken Sandwiches with Broiled Vegetables, 18
Quick Chicken Pot Pie, 58
Roast Chicken Spanish Style, 112
Thai Chicken with Basil, 48
Mustard
Dijon-Chicken Spirals, 110
Grilled Chicken Dijon Salad, 180

Mustard (*continued*)
Grilled Chicken with Pesto Sauce, 118
Honey-Mustard Glazed Chicken, 140
Marinated Mustard Chicken, 102
Mustard-Glazed Chicken Sandwiches, 142
Pepper Pasta with Chicken and Dijon Teriyaki Sauce, 90
Rotelle with Grilled Chicken Dijon, 76

O

Olives
Artichoke-Olive Chicken Bake, 54
Chicken Cacciatore, 152
Chicken Pesto Tortelloni, 132
Hot & Spicy Arroz con Pollo, 66
Spicy Chicken Tortilla Casserole, 56
One-Dish Chicken 'n' Rice, 62
One-Dish Chicken Bake, 158
One-Pot Chicken Couscous, 76
Open-Faced Chicken Sandwiches with Broiled Vegetables, 18
Orange
Barbecued Orange Chicken, 148
Chicken Breasts with Orange-Lime Sauce, 124
Chicken with Orange and Basil, 112
Grilled Chicken with Orange-Cilantro Salsa, 126
Honey Nut Stir-Fry, 42
Mandarin Chicken Salad, 24
One-Dish Chicken 'n' Rice, 62
Sweet and Sour Chicken, 48
Zippy Orange Chicken and Rice, 170
Oriental Chicken Cabbage, 18
Ortega® Chicken Fajitas, 90
Oven Chicken & Rice, 72

P

Pasta
Artichoke-Olive Chicken Bake, 54
Chicken & Pasta Toss with Sun-Dried Tomatoes, 84
Chicken and Vegetables with Mustard Sauce, 36
Chicken-Asparagus Casserole, 60
Chicken in Cream Sauce, 96
Chicken in Wine Sauce, 164

Pasta (*continued*)
Chicken Marengo, 166
Chicken Marsala, 78
Chicken Parmesan Noodle Bake, 140
Chicken Pasta, 92
Chicken Pesto Mozzarella, 108
Chicken Pesto Tortelloni, 132
Chicken Tetrazzini, 54, 66
Chicken Tetrazzini with Roasted Red Peppers, 84
Chili Pepper Pasta Santa Fe Style, 86
Creamy Herbed Chicken, 38
Drunken Chicken, 82
Easy Chicken Fettuccine, 178
Grilled Chicken Pasta Toss, 104
Honey-Lime Glazed Chicken, 150
Jiffy Chicken Supper, 88
Lemon Pepper Pasta with Chicken and Dijon Teriyaki Sauce, 90
Mandarin Chicken Salad, 24
Peppy Pesto Toss, 152
Rotelle with Grilled Chicken Dijon, 76
Southwest Skillet, 78
Spicy Chicken Salad in Peanut Sauce, 28
Spicy Mesquite Chicken Fettuccine, 176
Peaches
Santa Fe Grilled Chicken, 104
Sweet & Sour Cashew Chicken, 42
Peanuts: Kung Pao Chicken, 40
Peas (*see also* **Snow Peas**)
Chicken Tetrazzini, 66
Creamy Herbed Chicken, 38
Hot & Spicy Arroz con Pollo, 66
Spanish Skillet Supper, 142
Pecans: Warm Chicken and Rice Salad, 26
Peppers, Bell
Arroz con Pollo, 92
Artichoke-Olive Chicken Bake, 54
Barbecue Chicken with Cornbread Topper, 56
Barbecued Chicken Pizza, 162
Basil, Chicken and Vegetables on Focaccia, 12
Chicken and Andouille Gumbo, 23
Chicken and Asparagus Stir-Fry, 136
Chicken and Vegetables with Mustard Sauce, 36
Chicken-Asparagus Casserole, 60
Chicken Cacciatore, 174
Chicken in Cream Sauce, 96
Chicken Pasta, 92

Peppers, Bell (*continued*)
Chicken Primavera, 114
Chicken Provençale, 98
Chicken Salad Primavera in Pita, 20
Chicken with Walnuts, 34
Chili Pepper Pasta Santa Fe Style, 86
Creamy Herbed Chicken, 38
Creole Chicken, 86
Creole Chicken Thighs & Rice, 98
Curried Chicken Cutlets, 182
Glazed Chicken & Vegetable Skewers, 180
Indian-Spiced Chicken with Wild Rice, 62
Kung Pao Chicken, 40
Little Italy Chicken and Rice, 60
One-Dish Chicken 'n' Rice, 62
Ortega® Chicken Fajitas, 90
Peppy Pesto Toss, 152
Roast Chicken Spanish Style, 112
Sesame Chicken and Vegetable Stir-Fry, 182
Southwestern Style Stir-Fry, 46
Southwest Skillet, 78
Spicy Chicken Tortilla Casserole, 56
Sweet & Sour Cashew Chicken, 42
Sweet and Sour Chicken, 48
Szechuan Stir-Fry, 50
Tex-Mex Chicken Kabobs, 164
Warm Chicken and Rice Salad, 26
Zippy Orange Chicken and Rice, 170
Peppy Pesto Toss, 152
Persian Chicken Breasts, 168
Pesto Sauce
Chicken Pesto Mozzarella, 108
Chicken-Pesto Pizza, 144
Chicken Pesto Tortelloni, 132
Grilled Chicken with Pesto Sauce, 118
Peppy Pesto Toss, 152
Pineapple
Grilled Ginger Chicken with Pineapple and Coconut Rice, 160
Zippy Orange Chicken and Rice, 170
Pizza
Barbecued Chicken Pizza, 162
Chicken-Pesto Pizza, 144
Spicy Chicken Stromboli, 134
Pollo Verde Casserole, 64
Pork (*see also* **Bacon, Ham, Sausage**):
Country Chicken Stew, 96

Potatoes
Coq au Vin, 74
Glazed Chicken & Vegetable Skewers, 180
Roasted Chicken and Vegetables over Wild Rice, 52

Q

Quick-as-a-Wink Chicken, 156
Quick Chicken Pot Pie, 58

R

Radishes: Mandarin Chicken Salad, 24
Raisins
Indian-Spiced Chicken with Wild Rice, 62
One-Pot Chicken Couscous, 76
Reuben Chicken Melts, 154
Rice
Arroz con Pollo, 92
Chicken and Andouille Gumbo, 23
Chicken and Asparagus Stir-Fry, 136
Chicken & Rice Bake, 70
Chicken Cordon Bleu, 118
Chicken Curry, 80
Chicken Fiesta, 72
Chicken Fried Rice, 36
Chicken with Walnuts, 34
Country Chicken in Rich Onion Gravy, 128
Creole Chicken Thighs & Rice, 98
Glazed Chicken, Carrots and Celery, 168
Grilled Ginger Chicken with Pineapple and Coconut Rice, 160
Hot & Spicy Arroz con Pollo, 66
Indian-Spiced Chicken with Wild Rice, 62
Little Italy Chicken and Rice, 60
Minute® Easy Chicken Stir-Fry, 147
One-Dish Chicken 'n' Rice, 62
Oven Chicken & Rice, 72
Quick-as-a-Wink Chicken, 156
Roasted Chicken and Vegetables over Wild Rice, 52
Sesame Chicken and Vegetable Stir-Fry, 182
Southern-Style Chicken and Greens, 88

Rice (*continued*)
Southwestern Chicken Soup, 23
Spanish Skillet Supper, 142
Warm Chicken and Rice Salad, 26
Zippy Orange Chicken and Rice, 170
Roast Chicken Florentine, 106
Roast Chicken Spanish Style, 112
Roasted Chicken and Vegetables over Wild Rice, 52
Roasted Red Peppers: Chicken Tetrazzini with Roasted Red Peppers, 84
Roasted Rosemary-Lemon Chicken, 173
Rotelle with Grilled Chicken Dijon, 76

S

Salads
Caesar Chicken Salad, 158
Chicken Salad Primavera in Pita, 20
Gazebo Chicken, 14
Grilled Chicken Dijon Salad, 180
Mandarin Chicken Salad, 14, 24
Oriental Chicken Cabbage, 18
Spicy Chicken Salad in Peanut Sauce, 28
Summer Caesar Salad, 30
Warm Chicken and Rice Salad, 26
Warm Chicken Taco Salad, 32
Salsa
Arroz con Pollo, 92
Chicken and Black Bean Enchiladas, 68
Chicken Fajitas, 172
Chicken Santa Fe, 126
Ortega® Chicken Fajitas, 90
Pollo Verde Casserole, 64
Southwestern Style Stir-Fry, 46
Southwest Skillet, 78
Spicy Chicken Tortilla Casserole, 56
San Francisco Grilled Chicken Sandwiches, 28
Sandwiches
Basil, Chicken and Vegetables on Focaccia, 12
Caesar Chicken Sandwiches, 22
Chicken Salad Primavera in Pita, 20
Easy Oriental Chicken Sandwiches, 20
Mediterranean Chicken Salad Sandwiches, 32
Mustard-Glazed Chicken Sandwiches, 142
Open-Faced Chicken Sandwiches with Broiled Vegetables, 18

Sandwiches (*continued*)
Reuben Chicken Melts, 154
San Francisco Grilled Chicken
Sandwiches, 28
Thai Chicken Sandwiches, 16
Santa Fe Grilled Chicken, 104
Sausage
Chicken and Andouille Gumbo, 23
Chicken Fiesta, 72
Savory Chicken & Biscuits, 68
Sesame Chicken and Vegetable Stir-Fry, 182
Simple Marinated Chicken Breasts, 108
Snappy Chicken and Vegetables, 94
Snow Peas
First Moon Chicken Stir-Fry, 44
Grilled Chicken Pasta Toss, 104
Lemon Cashew Chicken Stir-Fry, 46
Oriental Chicken Cabbage, 18
Sesame Chicken and Vegetable Stir-Fry, 182
Soups
Chicken and Andouille Gumbo, 23
Chicken and Vegetable Chowder, 26
Chicken-Barley Soup, 24
Country Chicken Chowder, 30
Hot and Sour Soup, 16
Southwestern Chicken Soup, 23
Southwest White Chili, 22
Sour Cream: Pollo Verde Casserole, 64
Southern Fried Chicken, 110
Southern-Style Chicken and Greens, 88
Southwestern Style Stir-Fry, 46
Southwest Skillet, 78
Spanish Skillet Supper, 142
Spicy Chicken Stromboli, 134
Spicy Chicken Tortilla Casserole, 56
Spicy Mesquite Chicken Fettuccine, 176
Spinach
Roast Chicken Florentine, 106
San Francisco Grilled Chicken
Sandwiches, 28
Spicy Chicken Salad in Peanut Sauce, 28
Squashes
Basil, Chicken and Vegetables on
Focaccia, 12
Lemon Chicken with Walnuts, 82
Roasted Chicken and Vegetables over
Wild Rice, 52
Roasted Rosemary-Lemon Chicken, 173
Snappy Chicken and Vegetables, 94
Tex-Mex Chicken Kabobs, 164

Stews
Country Chicken Stew, 96
Mexicali Chicken Stew, 94
Mexican Chicken Stew, 80
Stuffed Chicken Breasts à la Française, 176
Stuffed Chicken with Apple Glaze, 100
Stuffing Mix
One-Dish Chicken Bake, 158
Stuffed Chicken with Apple Glaze, 100
Summer Caesar Salad, 30
Sweet & Sour Cashew Chicken, 42
Sweet and Sour Chicken, 48
Szechuan Stir-Fry, 50

T

Tangy Chicken Breasts with Citrus Sage
Sauce, 170
Tex-Mex Chicken Kabobs, 164
Thai Chicken Sandwiches, 16
Thai Chicken with Basil, 48
Tomatoes
Artichoke-Olive Chicken Bake, 54
Chicken Breasts Smothered in Tomatoes
and Mozzarella, 156
Chicken Cacciatore, 174
Chicken Fajitas, 172
Chicken Parmesan, 64
Chicken Parmesan Noodle Bake, 140
Chicken Pesto Mozzarella, 108
Chicken-Pesto Pizza, 144
Chicken Pesto Tortelloni, 132
Chicken Provençale, 98
Creole Chicken, 86
Creole Chicken Thighs & Rice, 98
Hot & Spicy Arroz con Pollo, 66
Little Italy Chicken and Rice, 60
Mexicali Chicken Stew, 94
Mustard-Glazed Chicken Sandwiches,
142
Roast Chicken Spanish Style, 112
Snappy Chicken and Vegetables, 94
Southern-Style Chicken and Greens, 88
Warm Chicken Taco Salad, 32
Tomatoes, Sun-Dried
Chicken & Pasta Toss with Sun-Dried
Tomatoes, 84
Chicken-Barley Soup, 24
Chicky Quicky, 150
Southwestern Chicken Soup, 23

Tortilla Chips
Mexicali Chicken Stew, 94
Pollo Verde Casserole, 64
Warm Chicken Taco Salad, 32
Tortillas
Chicken and Black Bean Enchiladas, 68
Chicken Fajitas, 172
Ortega® Chicken Fajitas, 90
Persian Chicken Breasts, 168
Spicy Chicken Tortilla Casserole, 56

V

Vegetables (*see also individual listings*)
Corny Chicken Pot Pie, 178
Minute® Easy Chicken Stir-Fry, 147

W

Walnuts
Chicken with Walnuts, 34
Lemon Chicken with Walnuts, 82
Oriental Chicken Cabbage, 20
Warm Chicken and Rice Salad, 26
Warm Chicken Taco Salad, 32
Water Chestnuts
Mandarin Chicken Salad, 24
Oriental Chicken Cabbage, 18
Sesame Chicken and Vegetable Stir-Fry,
182
Wine
Chicken Cacciatore, 174
Chicken in Wine Sauce, 164
Chicken Marengo, 166
Chicken Marsala, 78
Chicken Provençale, 98
Chicken with Orange and Basil, 112
Coq au Vin, 74
Country Chicken Stew, 96
Creole Chicken, 86
Drunken Chicken, 82
Lemon Chicken with Walnuts, 82

Z

Zippy Orange Chicken and Rice, 170

METRIC CONVERSION CHART

VOLUME MEASUREMENTS (dry)

1/8 teaspoon = 0.5 mL
1/4 teaspoon = 1 mL
1/2 teaspoon = 2 mL
3/4 teaspoon = 4 mL
1 teaspoon = 5 mL
1 tablespoon = 15 mL
2 tablespoons = 30 mL
1/4 cup = 60 mL
1/3 cup = 75 mL
1/2 cup = 125 mL
2/3 cup = 150 mL
3/4 cup = 175 mL
1 cup = 250 mL
2 cups = 1 pint = 500 mL
3 cups = 750 mL
4 cups = 1 quart = 1 L

VOLUME MEASUREMENTS (fluid)

1 fluid ounce (2 tablespoons) = 30 mL
4 fluid ounces (1/2 cup) = 125 mL
8 fluid ounces (1 cup) = 250 mL
12 fluid ounces (1 1/2 cups) = 375 mL
16 fluid ounces (2 cups) = 500 mL

WEIGHTS (mass)

1/2 ounce = 15 g
1 ounce = 30 g
3 ounces = 90 g
4 ounces = 120 g
8 ounces = 225 g
10 ounces = 285 g
12 ounces = 360 g
16 ounces = 1 pound = 450 g

DIMENSIONS

1/16 inch = 2 mm
1/8 inch = 3 mm
1/4 inch = 6 mm
1/2 inch = 1.5 cm
3/4 inch = 2 cm
1 inch = 2.5 cm

OVEN TEMPERATURES

250°F = 120°C
275°F = 140°C
300°F = 150°C
325°F = 160°C
350°F = 180°C
375°F = 190°C
400°F = 200°C
425°F = 220°C
450°F = 230°C

BAKING PAN SIZES

Utensil	Size in Inches/Quarts	Metric Volume	Size in Centimeters
Baking or Cake Pan (square or rectangular)	8×8×2	2 L	20×20×5
	9×9×2	2.5 L	23×23×5
	12×8×2	3 L	30×20×5
	13×9×2	3.5 L	33×23×5
Loaf Pan	8×4×3	1.5 L	20×10×7
	9×5×3	2 L	23×13×7
Round Layer Cake Pan	8×1½	1.2 L	20×4
	9×1½	1.5 L	23×4
Pie Plate	8×1¼	750 mL	20×3
	9×1¼	1 L	23×3
Baking Dish or Casserole	1 quart	1 L	—
	1½ quart	1.5 L	—
	2 quart	2 L	—